As I Remember It

My 50 Year Career
As An Award Winning Writer,
Producer, And Studio Executive

KEN ROTCOP

Published in the USA by:

BearManor Media

P O Box 71426

Albany, Georgia 31708

www.bearmanormedia.com

Printed in the United States of America

ISBN   978-1-62933-095-2 (paperback)

Book & cover design and layout by Darlene Swanson • www.van-garde.com

Dedication

THIS BOOK IS dedicated to Tyler Bohle, my grandson who lives in Berlin and hardly knows me, our meetings are so few and so far apart. I hope these stories will allow him to know his grandpa a little better.

****

I also dedicate this book to my audiences who have heard me speak on cruise ships.

I'm really not a lecturer. Lecturers teach. I think I entertain. I tell stories. Stories about Hollywood. As I remember it. Stories about celebs I've worked with, rubbed elbows with, and those who became friends.

Stories that evidently audience members wanted to share with others.

Evidently, after speaking, audience members would come up to me and ask where they could purchase these stories.

"Surely you've written them down in a book."

"Well, uh, actually no."

That is until now.

Thanks for asking.

Here are those stories.

What a wonderful life I've had!
I only wish I'd realized it sooner.

- Colette

Contents

Acknowledgements

TO MY LOVELY wife Connie, who kept the home fires burning, the soup hot in the kettle, the biscuits warm in the oven, and snuggled up with Kady our dog on our love seat in my office and watched and listened to me talking to myself, laughing, bickering, mumbling and crying while I burned the midnight oil.

To my wonderful assistant Brian Frederick, editor, and extension of my family, without whom I would be lost. He has made himself available to Connie and Kady and me 24/7. Without his help these words would still be in my head or written in pencil on yellow-lined paper sitting on my bookshelf. He keeps amazing me with his knowledge about EVERYTHING!

To my dear friend Dan Klein, who started an audio book publishing company and wanted this book for his first offering. Here it is, Dan. Go do your magic!

Introduction

MOST YOUNG PEOPLE come to Hollywood to be either actors or directors or writers.

They fail as actors.

They fail as directors.

They fail as writers.

So they become studio executives.

I was one of them.

If you were pitching a script to Avco Embassy pictures, or Hanna-Barbera, or Cannon Films, or TransWorld Productions you could have been pitching to me.

And if I turned your story down, remember what you called me after you left my office?

"Idiot!" You called me an idiot.

And as you'd walk down the hallways you'd mumble, "How did Rotcop get that job anyway? He's stupid, insipid, no-talent idiot!"

And, as your story got turned down all over town, it became obvious to you that all studio executives, not just Rotcop, all studio executives were idiots.

We just didn't get it! We didn't see the movie you saw. We only cared about the almighty dollar, not your great screenplay.

In short, we were all idiots!

****

But of the parade of writers who came to pitch their stories to me, and of the mounds of scripts I'd read, I began to get the courage to think that maybe I could start writing again.

Maybe I should give up the good life of the studio executive and take the risk, the gamble of writing on speculation.

Maybe my wife and I wouldn't go to Europe on vacation, and maybe my kids wouldn't wear designer label clothing, and maybe we'd have to pull back for a year or maybe two so I could try to write.

Maybe I'd hit it big. Or maybe I wouldn't. I was scared. We had a home in Bel Air and a couple of fancy cars and two kids and two dogs. What if our savings ran out while I was waiting to hit it big?

So I wrote. And rewrote. And rewrote again. And my script 'For Us the Living: The Story Of Medgar Evers' sold. And got made. And won awards.

Suddenly, this 'idiot' was an award-winning writer. Winner of, among the honors, the prestigious Writers Guild Award, the Neil Simon Award, and the Image Award.

And, I was featured on 'Oprah,' 'Starz Entertainment,' and on NPR's 'All Things Considered.' And I was written about in the Wall Street Journal, L.A. Times, and most of the writers' magazines.

In the beginning I wrote a game show, a documentary series, and Saturday morning animation but not dramatic scripts. In the beginning, I had no confidence.

Who the hell cared what I wrote? Who cared what I had to say? I mean there was Paddy Chayefsky, Stirling Silliphant, Rod Serling, and Ray Bradbury. They had something to say.

They were writers.

Did I have talent?

Maybe.

But so did a zillion other unemployed writers in Hollywood.

Writers waiting for somebody to discover their screenplays, waiting for someone to say, "Yes. Let's make this movie!"

They'd go to story meetings, agent meetings, manager meetings, producer meetings.

"Please read my script."

"Please listen to my pitch."

"Please hear my logline."

"Please look at me, hear me, read me."

And some broke through because of their talent. Some because of a connection. Some because they were persistent. And some made it because they got lucky.

I was one of the lucky ones.

✳✳✳✳

All of the stories you're about to read are titled with the names of celebrities. A few of them I never met, yet all of them, one way or another, impacted on my life.

NEW YORK

Mitch Miller

I WAS WORKING in advertising in New York but I really wanted to write screenplays. Problem was I didn't have a clue how to write them or what to do with them after I wrote them.

I bought a magazine on writing and the big advice they gave was, if you want to break into show business get to know other people in show business. Some advice! I didn't know anybody in show business so I threw the magazine into the trash.

Little did I know then that I was about to meet some of the biggest actors, directors, and writers!

****

I used to play softball in Central Park on Saturdays. On one Saturday two guys came over to me after the game and asked if I was available to play on their team on Thursday afternoons in an actors' league. It turned out their third baseman had moved to California and they were short of a third baseman.

I played third base.

That Monday, at the agency, I told my partner, Jerry Mandel, "Jerry, I got a chance to play softball in a league on Thursday afternoons. I have to meet these guys at two o'clock on Thursday in the men's room in Central Park and they'll give me my uniform."

"What *guys*?"

I shrugged. "I don't know. Guys."

"You're gonna meet some strange guys in the men's room in Central Park? What are you, nuts? Don't you know what goes on in the men's room in Central Park?"

I shrugged again. "They're gonna give me a uniform."

"Uniform?!" said Jerry. "Uniform?! They'll probably give you a dress!"

But of course, I went anyway and they did give me a uniform and it said 'Actors Studio' on the front and on the back it read 'Circle in the Square.'

And I asked, "What does that mean?"

"The Actors Studio is a workshop where actors go to study and we have our own theater called Circle in the Square. It's down in the village and we put on plays and you're going to play for our team."

Well, I gotta tell you it was a ball. We'd play every Thursday. Many of the Broadway shows and teams: 'West Side Story,' 'Bye, Bye Birdie,' 'The King and I.' I remember Lucille Ball coming out with her show, 'Wildcat.' And the stands were always packed with people who wanted to see the Broadway stars up close.

Now, remember I wanted to be a writer. There was one writer on the team. His name was Eliot Asinof and he had written a book called 'Eight Men Out' about the Chicago White Sox scandal and the 1919 World Series. It eventually became a movie.

So, after one of the games, I said to Eliot, "I would like to become a writer, any suggestions?"

And he said, "Well if I were you, I would go to NYU. There's a woman there named Michelle Cousin and I would take a writing course with her. She's very good and if she thinks you have talent she may help you get started."

∗∗∗∗

I've got to tell you about some of the players on the Actors Studio team. The pitcher was George C. Scott.

Second base was Arthur Penn. He had directed a lot of movies like 'The Miracle Worker,' 'Little Big Man,' 'Bonnie and Clyde,' and also Broadway plays.

The shortstop was Robert Loggia, who played in a lot of movies: 'Big,' 'Scarface' and 'Independence Day.'

The outfield was: Paul Newman in left, the centerfielder was Bruce Dern, the right fielder was Ben Gazzara, and the short centerfielder (we played with ten men those days) was Peter Falk.

We played every Thursday in the Broadway Show League and on Sundays the guys got together and we played chose-up sides.

I always remember when Paul Newman would come on Sundays, he would come with his kids and he'd march them into the park in order of their height, the tallest, the one in the middle, the little one, and behind them who I figured was the maid, in a house dress, wearing no make-up.

The kids would take off their jackets and leave them on the ground, then off came their sweaters, one was always dropping his baseball glove, another his sunglasses. And there was 'the maid' running around picking it all up.

It wasn't until she got in the stands that I realized 'the maid' was Paul's wife, Academy Award winner Joanne Woodward.

Anyway, because I played third base, I got to know showbiz people. Just like that magazine I threw away said I should! During our Sunday softball games, I noticed a really cute young lady with short blonde hair sitting by herself in the bleachers holding her dog, a mutt, and watching the game.

After the games I waited to see which one of the players she was going home with.

Actually it was none. She walked off into the park by herself, walking the dog. Same routine every Sunday.

April turned into May and she was always there by herself, watching the game then heading into the park, her little dog on a leash.

I was going back to my apartment to take a long, hot shower as I did every Sunday after the game. Then a couple of hours of practicing on my guitar, then maybe walk over to one of the delis for a sandwich.

✳✳✳✳

One day, instead of heading home, I took off after the blonde.

Catching up to her and her mutt, I introduced myself, told her I saw her at the game every Sunday, and if she didn't mind some company I'd like to walk with her.

She smiled and said, "You play third base." She knew who I was!

And so began our friendship. And for the rest of the summer, after the games, she and I and the dog took long walks through Central Park.

And every Sunday, when the sun would disappear behind tall, swanky apartment buildings on Fifth Avenue, she would leave me. She headed toward the 70s; I walked back to East 53rd Street.

We never went out for dinner or went to a movie or to an art gallery or even spoke on the phone during the week. We just meandered through the park and watched the kids ride the carousel, or fly their kites, or sail their toy boats on the Hans Christian Andersen Pond.

We watched families picnicking on the grass, or young couples walking hand-in-hand or old men sitting on benches reading their Yiddish newspapers or tossing peanuts to the pigeons.

We just walked. She held the leash and her purse, me with my mitt in one hand and my bat slung over my shoulder.

And we talked.

Not so much the first week but after when she began to know me and, I guess, trust me.

Her name was Tess. She was from a small town in Alabama. She came to New York for love? Adventure? A career? She didn't know. She just knew she wanted out of her small town in Alabama.

In New York she was invited to a party in one of those swanky Fifth Avenue apartments. She was maybe twenty-one, twenty-two. At the party she met an older man with a moustache and a Van Dyke beard. He asked her if she sang. She said no. She said she had just arrived in New York and was looking for a job.

He told her he had one for her.

She was excited.

The job was that he would set her up in an East Side apartment, give her money for clothes and food, and that from time to time he would come and visit her.

She told me she was confused. She asked, "That's all?"

"One condition," he said. "You must stay in the apartment and wait for my calls." He told her his schedule was complex and that he never knew when he would be available.

"After I visit with you," he went on, "You are free to do whatever you want for the next three hours. Go shopping, go to a movie, whatever. But then, get back in the apartment and wait for me to call."

And then with a smile he added, "Except Sundays. Sundays you are off. Go to the park, visit a museum, go to the theater. Whatever you want to do. You'll always have plenty of money so you can go anywhere, buy anything."

At first, Tess thought this man must be rich and lonely and just wanted some company. Someone to talk to. Maybe, she thought, he had a very stressful job or no immediate family.

She thought maybe she could try it for a little while. After all, what did she have going? Nothing. And she *was* running out of money.

So he set her up in a swanky apartment and very soon she began to realize what his visits meant. Sweet, cute, Tess from Alabama became this older man's mistress.

"He's a very nice man, really. And he's not rough with me or discourteous. For the longest time I knew nothing about him other than his name. But now I listen to his radio show."

"His radio show?" I asked.

"Every Sunday night. He interviews Broadway celebrities from some restaurant or something."

I almost dropped my baseball bat. "Is his name Mitch Miller?" I asked.

"You've heard of him?"

"You are Mitch Miller's girlfriend?"

"Not his girlfriend, silly, his mistress!"

Mitch Miller, besides this Sunday night radio show, had had his own TV show, "Sing Along With Mitch." He was a big shot at Columbia Records, conductor of his own chorale, and recorded numerous hit records and albums.

"How long have you . . . uh . . . had this position?"

"I don't know. Seven, eight months."

"You're happy?"

"I guess so. Know what he bought me for my birthday?"

"Uh, uh."

"The longest extension cord in the world so I can take my phone now into every room in the apartment and don't have to run anymore to catch the phone when he calls."

"Gee," I said sarcastically. "What a nice guy."

****

Soon the softball season ended. The grass in Central Park turned brown. The trees lost their leaves. The carousel was shut down.

And Tess? It was a blustery autumn Sunday but I thought I'd take a walk over to the ball field to see . . . well, if maybe Tess was sitting in the bleachers.

She was not. We had never exchanged phone numbers. I didn't know her last name. I didn't even know her dog's name. I remember asking her one day, "What's your dog's name?"

And her answer with a shrug was, "He has no name. I call him Mutt."

****

Come the next spring, with bat and mitt in hand, I couldn't wait to get out to the ball field.

But she never showed. Maybe she went back to that little town in Alabama. Maybe she got married. Maybe he didn't let her out on Sunday anymore.

****

But I remember how disappointed I was that one blustery autumn Sunday. I was sure she'd be sitting there, cuddling Mutt, maybe waiting for me to show up.

But the bleachers were empty. The wind blew newspapers and dry leaves around the pitcher's mound and over toward second base.

Snow was in the air. I could feel winter gathering itself out beyond center field, out beyond the tall apartment buildings on the West Side.

But no Tess.

And I missed her. I really, really missed her.

It got dark. I went back to my apartment. Got into my pajamas. Hopped into bed with my guitar. But instead of practicing I turned on the radio. Just in time to hear the Mitch Miller Show.

Peter Falk

ONE DAY I'M running from my apartment on 53rd Street to midtown Manhattan to meet my parents to go to the theater. I'm running because I'm late and it's drizzling, not really raining.

On Broadway I come to where there are these three movie theaters in a row and under the marquee of one of the theaters is the guy who played short centerfield for us, Peter Falk.

And he says, "Ken, Ken, am I glad to see you." And he grabs my arm.

"Peter," I say, "What? What are you doing here?"

"Jesus, do you have a twenty I can borrow?"

"Yeah," I say.

"I haven't eaten in two days."

"Yeah." I reach in and give him a twenty. I can't tell you how many twenties I gave to actors over the years. "I'll pay you back, I'll pay you back," Peter says. And off I run to the theater.

****

About a year later, almost to the day, I'm walking down Broadway. There's that movie theater where Peter Falk was waiting, waiting for the rain to stop. On the marquee it reads "Murder, Inc." starring Peter Falk. In one year he went from borrowing twenty dollars to becoming a movie star!

And I'm still waiting for my twenty dollars.

Michelle Cousin

TAKING ELIOT ASINOF'S advice I enrolled in a writing class at NYU with a teacher named Michelle Cousin.

She liked my writing, thought my stories had potential, and I'd walk her to the subway after class (I know, kissing up to the teacher!). But we became friends and decided to meet before class and have dinner at one of the many Greenwich Village restaurants. It became a weekly ritual for the length of the class.

One week, after dinner, I went to the cloakroom, got Michelle's coat and scarf and mine. We put them on and headed across a cold and windy Washington Square to the college.

When I reached into my coat pocket to get my gloves I discovered a business card, no name or company logo, just written in red lipstick 'call me' and a phone number.

"Okay, Michelle, very funny," I smiled. "Is that your phone number?" I asked.

"No, that is *not* my phone number."

"Then . . . who?" I still didn't believe her.

"You obviously have an admirer." Now she was smiling.

"I'll tell you what," she added. "After class we'll call her."

To which I replied, "How do we know it's a her?"

And that's how the conversation went as we walked into her classroom.

After class, with Michelle's prodding, we called.

Some young lady answered. I told her I found her card in my coat pocket.

She told me she was sitting near us at the restaurant, couldn't help overhearing our talking about movies and theater and scripts. She thought I sounded like someone she'd like to meet.

Michelle whispered in my ear, "Invite her for a drink!"

Convinced now that this wasn't a Michelle prank, I made a date with the voice on the phone to meet at the bar of the same restaurant a couple of nights later.

When I hung up I turned to Michelle. "You're coming with me!"

"Me? She doesn't want to meet me and, besides, you're too old to have a chaperone. She just wants to meet the young, dashing, glib, *bon vivant* that was having dinner with that terribly interesting and erudite older woman."

And so we met at the bar at the same restaurant. Her name was Sandy. She was nice. No sparks but a pleasant enough meeting. We sipped our drinks.

She excused herself to go to the ladies' room. When she left I decided to go to the men's room.

When I started back to the bar I just caught Sandy, out of the corner of my eye, in the cloakroom. She didn't see me. But I watched as she put business cards with a lipstick message in each man's coat pocket!

Twenty minutes later I was on the phone with Michelle.

"Guess what?" I started. "Every man's coat in the restaurant got a card!"

Again prodded on by Michelle, I wrote of Michelle, Sandy, and me. Just about the way you are reading it now.

I sold it to Greenwich Village magazine. They sent me a check I think for five dollars. My first sale.

****

Thanks to Sandy I had become a professional writer.

Mel Brooks

FROM HIS 'THE Producers' on Broadway to 'Blazing Saddles' and 'Young Frankenstein' in Hollywood to his 'Thousand Year Old Man' recording, he's probably one of the most beloved producers, actors, and writers in the entertainment industry.

The world loves Mel Brooks.

Except me. I hate Mel Brooks.

But, before we get to Mel Brooks, here's another Michelle Cousin story.

She and I became really good friends and she was very, very helpful in introducing me to people and getting me jobs that got me started in the industry.

One day Michelle said to me, "I've written letters to colleges across the country asking them if they had students in their writers' programs who had written scripts that would be indigenous to their part of the country and, if so, to send them to me. And, I've gotten about thirty scripts back," she said.

"From the thirty I've got eight that are dynamite, really good. One comes from Louisiana about the fishing industry and one from California about breaking into the movie business and one from Florida about the man who invented water skis.

I have an idea for a TV series called 'Images of America' with all scripts written by college students. I set up a meeting with ABC to go in and pitch the series but there's just one problem."

"What's that?" I asked.

"I'm too nervous to pitch."

"What are you talking about? You're Michelle Cousin. You teach at NYU. You've written scripts. You've been a successful writer."

She said, "I could never pitch but I hear you in the classroom, *you* can pitch. Would you do me a favor and go to ABC and pitch 'Images of America' for me?"

I said, "Well maybe we can go together."

"No, no, you go. If I go with you I'll just screw it up." Michelle had been so good to me, had taught me so much, how could I say no?

✷✷✷✷

So she hands me these eight scripts and on the day of the appointment I go to ABC and I'm taken to the top floor and I've got these eight scripts that I'm holding and I'm ushered past secretary after secretary after secretary until I come to my destination.

Huge wooden doors are opened to a large beautiful office with a huge table, and sitting behind the huge table are six or seven men.

I walked in with those eight scripts. I plopped them down on the table, I introduced myself, and I said, "I'm here for Michelle who couldn't make it today. I'm going to pitch you a series called 'Images of America,'" when suddenly the door of the office opened and in ran this short funny-looking guy with a raspy voice. I found out later he was a writer on the 'Sid Caesar Show.' His name was Mel Brooks.

He immediately sized up the room, he leaped up on the table, and he started to do an Irish jig singing Hava Nagila around the table. (I know it makes no sense but that's what he did!)

Before I knew it, he picked me out, jumped off the table, grabbed my arm, yanked me out of the chair, took the pile of eight scripts off of the table, and shoved them into my stomach. I was now holding the eight scripts as he led me out of the room, talking to me a mile a minute.

"It was so great of you to come in," I don't even think he stopped to take a breath.

"One of the best pitches we've ever heard and we're certainly going to take it into consideration and we loved the fact that you brought in these scripts all the way from Yonkers even though we're never going to read them, we still want you to know that it was very nice of you to bring them and on the way out make sure you close the door behind you. In fact, I'm going to walk out with you and I'm going to take you right to the elevator. I'm going to ring the elevator for you and you're going to go down the elevator and that's a wonderful concept you have. I don't know anyone who brings a pile of scripts to a meeting. Boy, what were you doing? Trying to sell the scripts by the pound?"

And he walked me past secretary after secretary after secretary until we got to the elevator and he rang for the elevator and the elevator was jammed with people and he continued the banter holding the elevator door open with his finger pressed on the button. (He now had an audience.)

"We're certainly going to take your scripts into consideration. As you know, every week we have a big meeting and all the scripts that come in during the week we take them, throw them up to the ceiling, and those that stick we buy. The rest we turn down. Yours, we ain't throwing. Too many. Too heavy. Nobody else would bring in a pile of scripts. But you did. And so we're definitely going to take that into consideration. Just don't call us, we'll call you. Thank you so much for coming in."

Everybody in the elevator was either laughing or dumbfounded.

He shoved me into the elevator and the next thing I know I'm on the sidewalk in front of ABC and that was my first experience pitching a script.

✳✳✳✳

And now you know why I hate Mel Brooks!

Michelle didn't think he was funny either.

Marilyn Monroe

A FRIEND MADE reservations for my wife and me at the Cal Neva Lodge on Lake Tahoe.

At the Reno airport we met George, who would be our driver for the next two weeks and take us anywhere we wanted to go.

The reason the hotel was called Cal Neva is because there was a line right down the middle of their swimming pool. On one side of the line is California, on the other side, Nevada. You can actually swim from California to Nevada and back!

Anyway, from the hotel, there were two cabins. And George told us our neighbors in the other cabin were Frank Sinatra, Marilyn Monroe, Peter Lawford, and his wife Pat Kennedy Lawford.

****

George said we had him until two in the morning, then he would work for the Sinatra group, getting them booze and food for them to enjoy in their cabin.

Then at six in the morning, his job was to hide in the shadows near the swimming pool to make sure that Marilyn didn't fall in and drown herself.

Because, every morning at six, she would leave her cabin and stand next to the pool, where she would look up at a hill just beyond the property. Every morning at six, Joe DiMaggio would stand on that hill and they'd stare at each other for five or six minutes, then she'd turn around and go back to her cabin.

And George was to make sure she didn't fall in the swimming pool. Evidently, she was always a bit tipsy for her morning 'visits.' In his own way, I guess DiMaggio was still looking out for her.

And according to George, she looked awful. Every morning she wore the same dirty, vomit-stained terrycloth robe, her hair tangled, make-up smeared on her face, and her eyes glazed and vacant.

And I guess her morning 'visits' with DiMaggio was his way of making sure she was okay. But was she, really?

DiMaggio had tried to stay at the Cal Neva, but management, not wanting trouble, asked him to stay in a motel about a mile away as their guest. And so he did.

He came up to Tahoe when he heard that Marilyn had gotten kicked out of the casino (the one night they cleaned her up) because she was so drunk she was falling all over herself and management escorted her and Sinatra and the Lawfords out of the hotel and back to the cabin.

DiMaggio, supposedly still in love with Marilyn, actually came to take her back to L.A. but couldn't get any closer to her than the hill overlooking the hotel's swimming pool.

✳✳✳✳

All of these stories we would get nightly from George, who would pick us up, take us to different restaurants for dinner, or to some of the other hotels or showrooms for their shows.

He'd have us tucked into our bed by midnight, then until six-thirty he would do Sinatra's bidding.

One evening he called our cabin.

"I can't pick you up tonight. You'll have to eat here."

"What's wrong?" I asked.

"Monroe's sick. Really sick. Sinatra wants her out of here immediately. His private plane is getting ready. I gotta take her to the plane. Sorry."

He hung up.

Sick?! Well, duh, no kidding. I had caught glimpses of her twice when she'd come out of the cabin, to get some fresh air, I imagined, and to look down at the blue-green lake.

I was on our veranda, saw it was her, waved and said "Hi." Once, she kind of smiled back, the other time she ignored me.

But both times she looked awful. Dark, dark circles, lipstick askew, mascara running down the corners of her eyes, hair a mess, and that dirty, stained robe.

And I said to my wife, "She's obviously not well, why doesn't somebody do something? Call an ambulance. Get her to a hospital. Or at least call in a doctor."

❊❊❊❊

The thing is, *they* are Legends. *They* are above reproach. *They* do things the rest of us wouldn't dream of doing. Talk about Legends . . .

❊❊❊❊

. . . Lee Walls was a friend of mine. He had been the right fielder for the L.A. Dodgers. He told me Sinatra would come into the locker room before the games and ask Lee for tips so he could bet on that day's game.

Lee would tell Sinatra what players had hangovers, who had fights with their wives, whose mistresses were cheating, who was disgruntled because he wasn't playing enough, and other juicy tidbits that Sinatra used to decide which side to bet on.

Lee told me when the season ended and he went back to his home in Palm Springs, there on his front lawn was the most expensive, brand-new Rolls Royce that gambling money could buy.

Wedged under the windshield wiper a card: "Thanks. F.S."

Who does those kinds of things? You? Me? Only Legends.

****

Then there was Candice Bergen, another Legend. She was making a movie for my company down in Mexico called 'Soldier Blue.' It was a western.

I got a call from her manager.

Him: "Candice wants you to buy her a horse."

Me: "What do you mean 'buy her a horse?'"

Him: "The horse she's riding in the movie."

Me: "Tell her to buy the horse herself. She's making enough money on the picture."

Him: "Why do you want to upset her? Buy her the horse."

Me: "I'll tell you what. We'll get her a horse up here."

Him: "You don't understand. She's in love with *this* horse. She only wants *this* horse."

Me: "You gotta put them in quarantine for six months. You can't just bring 'em up. And it's Mexico, forgodsake, who knows what kind of diseases the horse might have."

Him: "You want she should walk off the picture?"

Me: "Are you threatening me over a horse?"

Him: "She's in love. What can I do?"

Me: "I'll call my boss and get back to you."

So I called Joe Levine in New York.

Me: "Candice wants us to buy her a horse down in Mexico."

Levine: "Why?"

Me: "They're in love."

Levine: "She and the horse?"

Me: "She and the horse."

Levine: "Why can't she have an affair with one of the actors instead?"

Me: "Her manager says she'll walk if we don't buy her the horse."

There's a long pause on the other end.

Finally . . .

Levine: "Buy her the fuckin' horse."

✳✳✳✳

Who threatens like that? Legends, that's who. Candice got her horse.
Would you have carried on like that? Would I?

✳✳✳✳

Another time, David Janssen was making a movie for us in New York
called 'Generation.'

He was a huge star, having just come off 'The Fugitive,' a top, top TV series that ran for four years. Before going off to make the film, he hosted a tennis tournament in Las Vegas.

Between sets he and I sat and had a drink.

Janssen: "Ken, I want you to make provisions to get my limo and my driver to New York for the length of the shoot."

Me: "Why don't we pick up a limo and a driver in New York? Less hassle, less expense."

Janssen: "Yeah, but I really love my limo and I love my driver."

I'm thinking, *Again with the love. It's Candice Bergen all over again. Only this time it's a limo and driver!*

Me: "It's not in the budget, David, but let me check with Levine."

At least he didn't threaten to walk off the picture!

I could hear Levine sigh and finally cave in. "Get him his fuckin' driver and limo."

Who makes that kind of demand? Would you? Would I? Only the Legends.

****

Which leads me back to the Cal Neva Lodge and Lake Tahoe and Marilyn Monroe.

George, the driver, told us when next we saw him that he picked Marilyn up in front of the cabin. She was still in that filthy robe but had a blanket wrapped around herself. She was shivering and her face was wet with perspiration. She got in the back seat.

As George was about to leave, Lawford and his wife suddenly came running out and jumped in the limo. They evidently decided at the last moment to go back to L.A. with Marilyn.

Sinatra never came out.

When our vacation ended, and my wife and I went home, it was a couple of days later we heard on the radio, "Marilyn Monroe is dead." The report went on but my head was already over five hundred miles away. Back to Lake Tahoe, Cal Neva, and the two cabins next to each other on the lake.

I'd like to think if it weren't Marilyn Monroe, if it was just a neighbor in the next cabin that looked so sick, I might've called the front desk for a doctor. But it wasn't any neighbor. It was a Legend.

$$****$$

Legends are different from us.

But, why didn't Sinatra call? Or Peter Lawford? Or Pat Lawford? Or Joe DiMaggio? Or George?

Or me?

Hollywood

Monty Hall

WE WERE ON our honeymoon in Acapulco when I got a phone call from Wes Kenney. Wes was the best man at our wedding and he was also the director of an NBC game show called 'Your First Impression.'

"How'd you like to come back to Hollywood for two weeks and write our show?" Wes asked.

"Write your show?! It's a game show. They need a writer on a game show?"

"Every day you go to the home of a celebrity who's going to be on the next day and teach them how to play the game. Then you come back to the office and write the questions out for that celebrity to answer. It'll be fun and it's just for two weeks."

At that time I had a boutique-advertising agency in Manhattan and my new wife and I had picked out an apartment around the corner from the Guggenheim Museum on 89th Street off Fifth Avenue.

I can't tell you how disappointed my bride was when I told her we were going back to Hollywood for two weeks.

Even though we had met in New York, she was from L.A. and it meant two more weeks after she said her tearful goodbyes to her family and friends.

I informed my partner, Jerry Mandel at the ad agency, that I was going to be writing a game show for two weeks.

"They have writers on game shows?" he asked.

"Of course! Boy, you don't know nuttin'," I replied.

So we went to Hollywood, I met the celebrities, wrote the questions, and escorted the celebrities into the NBC building to the studio on the nights of the tapings.

The producer of the show was Monty Hall. I liked him a lot and we got along great.

Another man I liked was Nat Ligerman. Monty was class. Nat was a *Mensch*. I was never really sure what Nat's job was. I thought he was like an Associate Producer. But he seemed to spend a lot of time with Monty although they were totally different.

Monty was smooth. Nat was Brooklyn.

I'm having lunch with Nat one day and he asks, "Wanna know how Monty and I got together?"

"Sure."

"I used to own a dry cleaning business in the Village (Greenwich Village in New York). Many, many years: shirts, dresses, pants, ties.

"And Monty was one of my regular customers. He and his wife had moved down from Canada where he used to broadcast soccer games on the radio.

"He came to New York because he had some ideas for a game show, or maybe more than one, I forgot. But anyway, he'd make the rounds of the networks and nothing was happening.

"Welcome to *Rejection City*.

"Anyway, he'd bring in some clothes for cleaning and he tells me of one rejection after another. He was really down and I felt sorry for him.

"So I said to him, 'Monty, I have an idea for a game show.'

"Monty said, 'Forget it. It's too hard. They're not interested unless you're Goodson-Todman or Merv Griffin.'

"I said, 'Monty, just listen to the premise. Three panelists are seated - ' Monty cuts me off. Tells me to forget it. Besides, he says, he's got his own shows. This goes on for months. Monty brings in his laundry, I try to pitch him my idea. He tells me of his rejections. Finally, out of desperation, he listens to me.

"And guess what? That's the show he sold! That's how 'Your First Impression' got on NBC. Monty kept his word. He said, if he got lucky to sell my show I would be part of the package. When they decided to move the show to the West Coast, I got out of the dry cleaning business and with Shirley and the kids we moved to L.A. with Monty and Marilyn and his kids. And that's how I left dry cleaning and got into show business!"

That was Nat's story that day at lunch over tuna melts.

****

My story? After my two weeks were up, Monty asked me to stay with the show and offered me a contract. The writer who took the sabbatical was fired. I sold my share of our advertising agency to my partner Jerry.

My bride and I moved permanently to Los Angeles. Fifty years later and I'm still here.

As for the writer who took the two-week sabbatical? I guess we both learned you never take a vacation when you're on the staff of an ongoing show. We're all so easily replaceable.

And always listen to your dry cleaner when he says he has an idea for a show.

Regis Philbin

I MET AN agent at a party. He said he would call me if I heard of anything I'd be right for.

"Yeah, right," I figured.

But lo and behold, he called.

"CBS is starting a daytime 'Tonight Show'. Interviews, singers, comics, just like Johnny Carson only it's going on at noon. They're looking for a writer. Wanna go on an interview?"

"Are you kidding?! When?"

So a meeting at CBS was set up. I told my wife if she'd come with me I'd take her out to lunch after.

In the car we fought. Why? Susan, who was pregnant, didn't want to put on her seatbelt.

"Put it on!"

"I can't!"

"Why?"

"If I put it above the bump, it hurts my breasts."

"Then put it under the bump."

"Under the bump is no protection. Maybe I'll put it on the bump!"

I freaked out! "Don't put it *on* the bump! If I have to stop quick you'll choke the baby!"

So we argued all the way over. What to do with the damn seatbelt.

✳✳✳✳

I get to the meeting. The program director is a guy named Joe Sands.

He starts to tell me about 'The Noon Show.' They're still looking for the host but they've hired a three-piece band and it's going to be the first daytime variety talk show aimed at women.

"And one of the segments," Sands says, "will be where the host goes into the audience and asks the studio members the Question of the Day.

"Like for instance . . ."

He starts to hem and haw. "You know a question like . . ." He's stuck.

So I jump in. "Like whether a pregnant woman should wear a seatbelt on the bump, *over* the bump, or *below* the bump!"

"You're hired!" exclaimed Sands.

And that's how I got my first writing job in Hollywood.

Thank you, Susan.

But what an adventure it turned out to be!

They had the band and they had the writer, me. Now they needed to hire a host.

There were three prospects. Bill Keene had been a weatherman at CBS in Hollywood for years. He was a possibility. Viewers liked his easy style. Kind of guy you'd watch a ballgame with.

Second was a young man named Brian Adams. He had a daytime talk show in Sydney, Australia.

Joe Sands liked his accent, his beautiful suits, and, boy, was he handsome!

The third candidate was a young guy from San Diego who had a local interview show there. He was upbeat, funny, and had a cherubic Irish face. His name was Regis Philbin. Yes, *that* Regis Philbin. Only outside of San Diego, no one knew him.

Regis really wanted 'The Noon Show.' He came up from San Diego every week while we were still putting the pieces together.

And he and I bonded. Maybe he thought I had some leverage and could push him to be the host. I told him that I was just the lowly writer and had no *juice* at all. But despite that, the thing that tied us together was that both our wives were due within days of each other.

Joe Sands hired Brian Adams. He figured the women were going to love him just based on his movie-star looks.

And Regis? Disappointed, baffled, hurt.

****

Came the day of our first show. As I'm walking past Brian Adams' dressing room on the way to the sound stage, a hand reaches out and yanks me into Brian's dressing room.

It's him . . . and he's panicked!

Sweat rains down from every pore.

His beautiful suit soaked. The flower he is wearing in his lapel has wilted and is drooping.

He pins me against the wall. He looks crazed.

"Don't let me down, Ken. I'm counting on you."

"Brian, you're sweating on me."

"I've dreamed of this day my whole life. Hollywood! I've made it, Ken, but I think I'm going to throw up."

"Not on my sweater, please, Brian, the sink."

Instead, he just swallowed whatever bile came up into his throat because I don't think he wanted to let go of me.

"Brian, I've written out the questions. They're on your desk on the set. Just follow the questions and you'll be fine."

"You think so?"

"I *know* so. Now go wipe your face and put on another beautiful suit, this one's beginning to smell from perspiration."

✳✳✳✳

The set was just like Leno's or Letterman's. Host's desk, guest's chair, sofa.

Our first guest was Debbie Reynolds.

Remember, Brian had the questions all written out for him on the desk.

Here's how the interview went, as I best remember it.

Brian: "It's a pleasure to have you as my guest, Debbie. I must say that I loved you in 'The Unsinkable Molly Brown.'"

Debbie: "Brian, I want to first apologize for the blood on my blouse and skirt. But there was a sixteen-car pileup on the freeway. We were, fortunately, right behind it. I ran out of the car. There was a woman lying on the freeway. Her head was bleeding. I held her in my lap till the ambulance came. I don't know if she made it."

Brian: "And I loved you in 'Singin' In The Rain.'"

I don't think Brian heard one word of Debbie's story.

He was so nervous, so focused on the next question on the desk, that he shut out everything around him.

The opening show was a disaster. He never listened to the guests, just read off my lists of questions.

After the show Brian went off somewhere to contemplate suicide.

The rest of us, the production team, was called immediately into the producer's office for an emergency meeting.

Our first show and already panic had struck 'The Noon Show.'

The producer, sitting behind his desk, pulled out a Johnny Walker bottle wrapped in a plain brown bag and was doing his best to get drunk.

The associate producer, a Latino lady (hired under the one-minority-per-show mandate) was blabbering away at me in Spanish.

And the director was rubbing my leg up and down and telling me everything was going to be all right.

My first production meeting, one show in, and already the thinking was we could be cancelled by Wednesday!

****

Somehow we limped through week after week. Brian Adams was getting no better.

Besides wearing flop-sweat on his beautiful suits he now, visibly, had the shakes. And every week Regis came up from San Diego.

"He's awful, Ken, get rid of him. Give me a shot. Let me at least come on as a guest."

"Regis, I spoke to the producer. I said put this guy on as a guest. He's funny, he's interesting. But the producer says nobody knows who you are. Reg, look at our guest list. This is Hollywood. We get the biggest names in show business. They love coming in at noon."

Poor Regis. He was so dejected. But that was nothing compared to the next time I saw him.

He didn't come up the next week. And I figured Kay (Regis' first wife) had had her baby. And like clockwork Susan (my first wife) had little redheaded Kimberly.

The following week Regis came up but he looked terrible. He came into my cubbyhole and plopped himself down.

"Regis, what's wrong?"

He forced a smile.

"Your wife have her baby?"

"Yeah. A girl. A redhead! Kimberly Sue."

"Baby okay?"

"Yeah. Ten fingers, ten toes." I paused, then, "Regis? What's wrong? Is Kay . . .?"

"Kay's fine. We have a boy, Daniel."

"Mazol Tov."

"No Mazol Tov. The little guy's spine is screwed up. He's missing some vertebrae and his legs . . ."

He had trouble going on.

"And his legs?" I asked.

"They're screwed up too. They've got to be amputated. Both of them. He'll be in a wheelchair his whole life."

We sat in that cubbyhole for a long time. Neither of us spoke. I mean, what was there to say? I couldn't look at him. I knew he was hurting and, looking back, maybe I should have gone around the desk and hugged him . . . or something. But I didn't.

Suddenly the phone rang.

It was Susan. I could feel her excitement through the phone.

"I just had to call. I was holding Kimberly and, I swear, she smiled. Not a burp, a real smile!" I looked at poor Regis sitting opposite me. I told Susan I'd call her back. Regis stopped coming up after that.

After thirteen weeks we were not cancelled but Brian was fired and sent back to Australia.

I was sure they'd hire Regis. The thinking was we should try a totally different look. Rather than hire another young host like Brian Adams, go for the more mature, middle-aged nice guy, the weatherman Bill Keene.

I didn't see Regis again. I left him a message: "I told you I had no juice."

Almost half a century has passed.

Regis? I hear he got work.

My daughter Kimberly lives in Berlin with her German husband, Stephan, and their eight-year-old son Tyler, a future soccer player for the German national team. They have a good marriage and both Kimberly and Stephan have successful careers and Tyler goes to the bilingual John F. Kennedy School.

And then there's Daniel, Regis' son. Confined to a wheelchair he nevertheless worked for the Department of Defense in Washington and was married.

He is sitting at his desk at the Pentagon on September 11, 2001, when American Airlines flight 77 smashed into the building. Daniel was one of the fortunate ones. He got out with his life.

Daniel was one of sixteen people with disabilities honored by the Department of Defense.

He was presented a citation that read:

"That evening, while the building was still in flames, Daniel Philbin returned to the Pentagon to help with the Secretary of Defense's press conference. He came back on September 12th to perform additional duties. The bravery and dedication were not without cost as he was later hospitalized for several days."

****

How proud Regis must have been for his son confined to a wheelchair.

Bill Keene did a great job on 'The Noon Show' and we lasted two years. I knew they were happy with my work. They gave me a larger cubbyhole.

Medgar Evers

WHEN THE SHOW ended, Joe Sands, the executive who had hired me to write 'The Noon Show,' called me into his office and immediately offered me another job. Actually, offered me a shot at another job.

"We're going to be doing a documentary series based on Black America history. We have an all-black staff, black producer, black director, black crews. But frankly we had to fire the writer, who wasn't very good. Interested?"

Was I interested?! Of course I was interested!

"You know much about Black American history?" Joe Sands asked.

"Do I know much about Black American history?!"

"Do you?"

"No."

"I'm not sure they even want a white guy but I set up a meeting. Right now they are so desperate they may not have a choice." The very next day I met the black producer and the black director.

They both gave me the Sonny Liston stare. Sonny Liston was the black heavyweight boxing champion that would stare down his opponents with such anger and hatred that the opponent was beaten before the fight even started.

That's how these guys looked at me. If looks could kill, I was dead.

Without saying a word I could hear them thinking, "What you doin' here, white boy?"

So the interview began.

"We want to do a show on Harlem. What do you know about Harlem?"

Having lived in New York for a number of years I knew something about the history of the city and that at one time Harlem was the garden spot of Manhattan and that the wealthy New Yorkers would ride their horse and buggies up to Harlem for Sunday picnics with their girlfriends or their families.

So far so good.

"We want to do a show on Martin Luther King and also one on Medgar Evers. Of course you know who Medgar Evers was?"

Being a sports fan, I jumped in with, "Wasn't he the second baseman on the Chicago Cubs? That famous double-play combination Tinkers to *Evers* to Chance?"

Silence.

"No, Medgar Evers was *not* the second baseman for the Chicago Cubs!"

They looked at each other then gave me my second dose of the Sonny Liston stare.

"If you want this job you come back here tomorrow and you tell us who Medgar Evers was!"

"Yes, sir. Uh, sirs. Yes, sirs."

* * * *

So, off to the library I went (no computers in those days). There was one book on Medgar Evers written by his widow Myrlie Evers. I read the biography that night. And I cried. Cried for this man, this civil rights leader, who was assassinated by a redneck, Byron De La Beckwith.

Medgar was running the NAACP in Jackson, Mississippi. He was killed because he was trying to integrate the public schools, or maybe because he was trying to get the blacks out to vote, or he was killed for forcing Woolworth's Five and Dime store to allow blacks to eat at the counter. De La Beckwith hid in the bushes and when Medgar came home one night he was gunned down in front of his house.

And when the ambulance came the question was would they take a dying black man into an all-white hospital.

It didn't matter. He died in the ambulance.

The next day I went back to the producer and director and with eyes still red from crying, recounted the story of Medgar Evers.

And got the job.

After 13 weeks as the writer on the series 'Images And Attitudes' we won the Image Award as the best new documentary series on television.

I guess the white guy did good.

****

A year later I wrote the screenplay for the dramatic version of Medgar's life titled after Myrlie's book, 'For Us, The Living: The Story of Medgar Evers.' It starred Howard Rollins, Laurence Fishburne, Irene Cara, Paul Winfield, Roscoe Lee Browne, and Margaret Avery.

I won numerous awards for writing and producing the story, including the prestigious Writers Guild Award, voted on by my peers. Most television critics called it the best TV movie of the year.

And here I thought Medgar was the second baseman for the Chicago Cubs!

Stan Lee

SOMEBODY BROUGHT A comic book into my office. "You should read this comic. It's really different."

So, as the creative head of Cannon Films, I spent my afternoon reading a comic book about a naked guy all in silver who couldn't walk and could only fly around on his surfing board. His name was Silver Surfer and he came from another planet or another dimension or another galaxy (I'm not at all hip when it comes to science fiction).

But the character was the most erudite and the story exciting, clever, and relevant. It would make for a great movie or at least an animated TV series. The story was longer than a comic book. The cover was of a thick, higher quality paper. It was bound more like a book than a comic book. It was the world's first *graphic novel*!

✳✳✳✳

I called Marvel Productions and spoke to Silver Surfer's author, Stan Lee. Stan Lee was a giant in the comic book world. He had created Spiderman, Hulk, Iron Man, Thor, and on and on.

I asked him if Silver Surfer was available for motion pictures and television.

"Too late, Mr. Rotcop, I've already made a deal with a producer for Silver Surfer."

"Oh," I said disappointedly.

"But, Captain America is available."

"Captain America?"

"Yes," said Stan Lee. "He really wasn't dead."

"I didn't even know he was sick," I admitted, not having read a comic since sixth grade. So I got what I thought might be a bright idea. "Mr. Lee, could you send over a poster of Captain America? My boss is Israeli and might not know of the heroic Captain."

So the next day I'm staring at a poster on my desk of a costumed character and I'm thinking, how am I going to sell this to my boss, Menahem Golan?

I go into Menahem's office and hold up the poster.

"Menahem," I had no idea where I was going. "You, of all people, should make this movie!"

My Israeli boss studied the poster. The Captain was in a fighting stance, fist cocked, ready to do damage to some anti-American foe. Dressed in his blue costume, a hood covering half his face with an 'A' above the eyes, and a red, white, and blue shield in his other fist, the Captain was ready for action!

And so was Menahem. "Let's do it!" he orders.

So I call up Stan Lee and we set up a lunch date to talk about Captain America and what the story for the movie should be.

✳✳✳✳

At lunch we talk about cabbages and kings and many things. He's a man of many interests. But when I asked him about his roster of characters, he gave me a lesson on the comic book industry and why he was so successful.

Before Stan, almost all comic book superheroes were perfect straight arrow people with no flaws or complexities. Stan, who *really* wanted to write serious novels, thought that he could make these comic book heroes more interesting if he gave them flaws or gave them complexities. So, Spiderman had fits of melancholy, and Hulk had a bad temper, and the X-Men bickered among themselves, and others worried about girlfriends and paying their bills and being bored with life.

In other words, Stan Lee took a risk and made superheroes with human frailties. And it worked. Stories became infinitely more interesting because the characters were infinitely more interesting. Stan Lee, the innovator, changed the face of comic books and brought in a more mature, older audience while holding on to the preteens.

That wasn't a lunch we had. It was a psychology lesson!

$$\star\star\star\star$$

Captain America, the movie, was made in Yugoslavia. After numerous rewrites the final story was so convoluted that it was next to impossible to follow. The picture got universally panned. Entertainment Weekly called it "a shapeless blob of a plot". I didn't think it was that good.

$$\star\star\star\star$$

I remember being at Stan Lee's Christmas party. No one, to the best of my knowledge, talked about the film. Instead, a good time was had by all.

I received a Christmas card from Stan that had drawings of all his characters around the message of goodwill towards men and, of course, Stan and his wife signed it.

I showed the Christmas card to my friend, who collected comic books and whose attic was filled with first editions and every issue of everything from Mickey Mouse Comics to Archie to Superman to who-knows-what-else.

"You want the card?" I asked as I saw his jaw drop.

"Are you kidding?! Do have any idea what this card would be worth?! I could take this to Comic-Con or put an ad in a collector's magazine. Do you have any idea what I could get for a card with Spidey and Hulk and Iron Man and Thor and Stan Lee's autograph?!"

Before he could go on gushing I picked up the phone and made a call.

"Hello Stan? It's Ken. Could you do me a favor? Could you send over about six more Christmas cards?!"

John Cassavetes

WHEN I WORKED for Cannon Films, Menahem Golan hired me because I was an award-winning writer and he was trying to get into television. So he wanted me to help him even though he was making a fortune with those low-budget features they cranked out.

So he said to me one day, "I'm building for you a cabin." What he meant was a cabinet.

He was an Israeli and his English sometimes got mixed up. "I'm building for you a cabin . . ."

I corrected him, "You mean a cabinet?"

"Yes, a cabinet so you can bring your awards in and we will put them in the cabinet. We will lock it up at night so nobody should steal from it and we'll have them here. It'll be nice you should have them in your office."

So I brought them in. And every time Menahem had a guest he would bring the guest into my office and say, "Here are some of the awards *we've* won. Here is the Writer's Guild, the Image Award, the Neil Simon Award." What he was doing was making it sound like the studio had won these awards. Though in truth, the studio had nothing to do with them. But because he could show the awards off, I became his pet.

It was all fine and good except we got very, very busy at the studio and John Cassavetes was going to make a movie there and there was no room. Literally no room for him. So one morning I came into the studio to go to my office and my desk was out in the hallway.

And I look in and there is Cassavetes sitting at a desk in *my* office with all *my* hardware behind him.

"John, what are you doing here?"

"Menahem thought I should have your office. Sorry."

✸✸✸✸

And that was it. From then on I sat out in the hallway. That night I took my awards out of the 'cabin' and brought them home. If I'm going to be taking meetings out in the hallway at least let me have the dignity of keeping my own statues!

E.B. White

LET ME TELL you how we stole 'Charlotte's Web' from Walt Disney.

Word had gotten out that E.B. White had gotten on in years and was ready to sell his classic book 'Charlotte's Web' for a movie.

The bidding war came down to the Disney Studios and Hanna-Barbera.

Joe Barbera, besides being a creative genius, was a terrific sales-man. But he couldn't convince E.B. White to sell the book rights to him.

So, out of frustration, Joe asked me to intervene. I was creative head of the studio at the time. I sat in my office staring at the phone wondering what I would say. Finally, I called E.B. White at his home in New England.

"Hello."

"Mr. White?"

"Yes."

"My name is Ken Rotcop. Joe Barbera asked me to give you a call."

"Mr. Rotcop, I don't want to waste your time. I've made up my mind to go with the Disney offer."

"Well I can certainly understand that. I certainly loved Walt Disney's 'Cinderella' and Disney's 'Bambi' and Disney's 'Snow White.'"

"If you're trying to get me to change my mind, Mr. Rotcop, you're not doing a very good job."

"Well, Mr. White, here is my point. If they make the movie it will forever more be known as Walt Disney's 'Charlotte's Web.' But, sir, if we make the move it will be for all eternity known as E.B. White's 'Charlotte's Web.' In all of the print ads, or the trailers, on the posters, all the publicity, and of course, in the movie itself. Not Disney's 'Charlotte's Web' or Hanna-Barbera's 'Charlotte's Web'. It will forever be known as E.B. White's 'Charlotte's Web.'"

There was dead silence on the other end of the line. Then, "Have Mr. Barbera send me a contract."

We made the movie. It was a smash hit. And that's how we stole 'Charlotte's Web' from Walt Disney.

My favorite pitch.

Mickey Mantle

WHEN I MOVED out to Los Angeles I found out there was a Hollywood Entertainers Softball League with teams sponsored by Jim Garner and Bobby Darin among other celebrities.

Since all the teams were filled and I knew none of the players I was told the only way to get into the league was to start my own team and get a celebrity to sponsor it. And we had two weeks to do it before the schedule started.

I scoured playgrounds and parks and softball fields and put posters up at the Directors Guild and the Writers Guild looking for ballplayers. You have to be in one of the entertainment unions or guilds to qualify for a team.

****

I pulled fifteen guys together. No try-outs, no auditions. Just show up and play. But now I had five days to get a sponsor.

One of the guys on the team was having a beer one night in Hollywood at a restaurant and sitting at the bar was Aldo Ray. Aldo had starred in a number of war movies such as 'Men In War', 'The Naked And The Dead' and 'The Green Berets'. So he approached him and said, "Mr. Ray, how would you like to sponsor a team in the

Hollywood Entertainers' League?" And that's how Aldo Ray became our sponsor and he came to every game. He was really great.

One of the league rules was that all the players had to be in the movie industry. There was a good-looking muscular guy in his 30s who came to one of our tryouts. He said he's going to be joining one of the labor unions to become a grip or best boy that would make him eligible to play on our team.

When I met him I asked, "Have you played any ball?" And he said, "Yeah, I played a little."

So I introduced myself and told him my name. And he said, "My name is Ken Hunt."

****

Ken Hunt had been the centerfielder for the Los Angeles Angels. Before that he played with the Yankees but the Yankees had a young kid named Mickey Mantle and they sold Kenny to the Angels. He was now retired and he became our centerfielder. He also became a good friend. I was always asking him to tell me stories of when he played in the big leagues.

****

One of the funniest stories he told me was when he was with the Angels and they went into New York to play the Yankees in a three game series. It was Friday, Saturday afternoon, and a single day game on Sunday. Friday they got to New York and it was pouring rain.

Kenny Hunt was staying at a hotel with the team when he got a phone call from his friend Mickey Mantle. Mickey said, "What are you doing tonight, Kenny? We're rained out."

Kenny said, "Eli Grba and I thought we go get a bite to eat."

So Mickey said, "Come up to my place. I'll get some food. We'll kill some time together."

Mickey was living in a swanky hotel across from Central Park. Kenny Hunt and Eli Grba, who was a pitcher on the Angels and also a former Yankee, went up to Mickey Mantle's suite.

What Mickey didn't tell Kenny was that not only did he have a dinner waiting but also he had hot and cold running women coming in and going out every hour on the hour. Kenny said that the food, booze, and women didn't stop until about four or five in the morning when they all fell asleep. Kenny was on the couch, Mickey was on the floor and Eli passed out on Mickey's bed.

Saturday it continued to pour so Mickey said, "Stay over. We'll party tonight," and they partied again Saturday night. Women coming in, food coming in, drinks coming in, and they were all plastered and drained.

Then it came Sunday and the weather cleared up and they all took a cab to Yankee Stadium. Mickey went his way into the Yankee locker room; Eli and Kenny Hunt went into the Angel locker room.

Bill Rigney, the manager, turned to Eli, who was so drunk he could hardly see straight, and said, "Eli, you're pitching the first game of the doubleheader."

Eli protested, "It's not my turn to pitch."

Rigney said, "Because of the rainouts we're changing things around. We're playing a double-header and you're pitching the first game."

****

So Eli went out to the pitcher's mound and as he was warming up he could hardly make out home plate. First batter up, and Eli walked him on four pitches. The second batter also walked on four pitches. The third batter got up and fouled off a couple of pitches. Eli said, "Thank God," and finally he walked him. The bases were loaded, nobody was out, and here came Mickey Mantle.

Bill Rigney ran out to the mound, "Eli, what are you doing? Throw the ball over the plate."

"Don't worry about a thing," Eli said. "You see who the batter is? If you think I'm drunk this guy's twice as plastered as I am. Don't worry about a thing."

Mickey came out from the men's room . . . he didn't even come out from the dugout, he came out from the men's room. His fly was still open and Eli thought that was hysterical and he said to Rigney, "Look, look how drunk this guy is. He didn't even zip up his fly." Rigney said, "Go get him."

Rigney went back into the dugout, Eli threw a pitch, and Mickey Mantle, drunk, hammered, and cockeyed, hit a grand slam homerun. "I mean," said Kenny Hunt, "he hit a mile!"

Before his death, Mantle was reported as saying, "I wonder how good I could have been if I played sober."

Thanks, Kenny Hunt, I always loved that story.

John Drew Barrymore, Jr.

WHEN I WAS creative head of AVCO Embassy Pictures we had our west coast offices in one of the tall office buildings in Century City. We were way up on one of the top floors and I remember we had floor to ceiling windows in all the offices with great views all the way to the Pacific Ocean. (But only on the clear days when there was no smog. Must have been about 7 or 8 days during the year you could actually see the blue water.)

✻✻✻✻

One day the receptionist calls me. "There's a John Barrymore here to see you." John Barrymore? At that time he'd been dead for over 40 years. It was just eerie hearing that name. Then I realized it must be his son.

We had announced that we had hired James Poe, the writer, to do a screenplay version of the biography 'Goodnight, Sweet Prince: The Life and Times of John Barrymore' by Gene Fowler and, I figured, the son was coming in to offer his services should we need any additional information.

Into my office the receptionist ushered the son of the great Broadway and Hollywood actor. This Barrymore, maybe in his late 20s at the time, was wearing a stretched out, soiled sweater, torn overalls, and bare, dirty feet. His hair was unkempt and his beard was scraggly.

He looked like a wild man. I found out quickly that he *was* a wild man.

"Are you Ken Ratcrap? Or Rottencrap? Or-"

"It's Rotcop. Ken Rotcop. And you are?"

"Barrymore. John Barrymore."

"Junior?"

"Yeah, Junior. What's it to you?"

He was belligerent, aggressive, and combative. And he was either drunk or stoned or both.

He walked towards me, his smelly, dirty feet on my new carpet (I didn't actually smell his feet, I just assumed) until his whisky breath was practically nose-to-nose with me. (His breath I could smell.)

Then he spat out this sentence: "Your face, Mr. Rattap, is the face that has killed and mutilated the baby of art!"

Before I could figure out what the hell he meant, he pushed me. Pushed me toward those floor-to-ceiling windows high above Century City.

I gasped, "What the fuck you doin'?!"

He grabbed me around the throat. I envisioned the two of us crashing through the glass together and him choking me to death before we both splattered over the Century City sidewalk.

I couldn't pull his hands apart. His whisky breath and his huge, bloodshot eyes were all I remember smelling and seeing. We were next to my desk. No, I did not grab a pen off the desk and jam it into his eye (actually I did in my daydreams days later).

My chair was on wheels and what I did was grabbed the chair by one of the arms and whipped the chair so it smashed into his leg. He released the grip on my neck to push the chair away. I shoved him and ran for the door.

Some of the guys in adjoining offices came running out and by the time I finished telling them my story, Mr. John Barrymore, Jr. was stumbling out the reception area and down the fire escape stairs.

I knew his coming up to our offices had something to do with our announcing that we were going to do his father's story. Outside of his making fun of my name, however, I haven't a clue why he chose to visit.

****

We never made the John Barrymore story. As good a writer as James Poe was, the script just didn't work and the project was abandoned. I can honestly say abandoning it had nothing to do with Junior.

Same day, that night. I'm driving home when over the radio I hear a car crashed on the way to Palm Springs. The driver was rushed to the hospital where he was in critical condition. The driver was John Drew Barrymore, Jr.

The newscaster went on to say that he had had numerous run-ins with the police and had been jailed a number of times for drunkenness, drug use, and spousal abuse. And though he had appeared in a number of movies and TV shows, he had recently dropped out, become a recluse, and was living the life of a hippie.

The accident didn't kill him but in 2003 he died of cancer. I read that his daughter, the actress Drew Barrymore, though estranged from him, took care of him and paid his bills until his death.

When I think back about my run in with Junior I can still hear him saying to me, "Your face, Mr. Rattrap, is the face that has killed and mutilated the baby of art!"

Huh?

Peter O'Toole

WHEN I WAS creative head of Avco Embassy Pictures, we bought a book called 'The Ski Bum' by Romain Gary.

Peter O'Toole read the book and committed to play the lead and it was decided to shoot the picture in London at the Pinewood Studios.

While the script was being written, my boss Joseph E. Levine had elaborate sets built, bringing in tons and tons of fake snow along with building a ski lodge, fake evergreen trees, ski slopes and mountains and cabins and making everything on the soundstage look like a great Swiss ski resort.

I was one of the first to get the completed screenplay. It was dreadful. I called Levine in London. "I don't think Peter O'Toole is going to like this script, Mr. Levine."

He grumbled something back to me (in those days overseas connections weren't as clear as nowadays).

So, ignoring my warning, script in hand, Joe walked from the Dorchester Hotel over to wherever Peter was staying and handed him the screenplay. Peter said he'd read it right away and told Joe to come back in a couple of hours.

When Joe came back, the first words out of O'Toole's mouth were, "I'd say this script is bloody awful. Surely you agree, Joe."

Peter said that under no circumstances would he make this picture. It needed a page one rewrite and even then . . .

But Joe couldn't afford a major rewrite, which could take months, maybe years. He was paying rent on a soundstage filled with tons of phony snow, a ski lodge, fake evergreen trees, ski slopes, mountains, cabins, and who-knows-what-else.

Despite Joe Levine's pleading O'Toole was adamant. Joe left despondent. What the hell was he going to do? At best he figured he was ruined.

Now, this is the way the story was told to me.

Joe wandered the side streets of London praying he wouldn't run into anybody he knew, it would be too embarrassing. And wouldn't you know it, he ran smack into Martin Poll, an American producer he knew from New York.

"Joe, what are you doing here?"

"I just came from Peter O'Toole." And Joe proceeded to tell Marty the story.

As the two of them stood there in the cold and the impending London fog, Joe asked Marty what was he doing in London.

"I'm walking the streets like you. I'm trying to sell a screenplay based on a play I bought. Nobody in the States was interested. I mean I couldn't even get anybody to read the script."

Joe remembered. "I saw that play. I thought it was pretty good." Suddenly Joe's eyes lit up. "You got a copy with you?"

Marty reached into the pocket of his overcoat and pulled out a rolled up copy. "It's not a fresh copy."

"So what," said Joe. "I want Peter O'Toole to read it."

Joe did not stop to read the script. Instead, he rushed back to O'Toole's hotel.

"Forget 'Ski Bum,'" Levine told O'Toole. "I hate 'Ski Bum!' But *this* script you gotta read!"

Peter unrolled the script and read it. "Can you get me Katie Hepburn to play opposite me?"

Because two American producers, despondent, down on their luck, happened to run into each other on a side street in London, one of the greatest movies ever made was born: 'The Lion in Winter.'

At least, that's the way the story was told to me.

And 'Ski Bum?' It got made. It got released. And it bombed. You can look it up.

Ray Bradbury

RAY BRADBURY IS best known for his novels 'Fahrenheit 451,' 'The Illustrated Man,' 'The Martian Chronicles,' and 'Something Wicked This Way Comes.'

I met him when he spoke at a Writers Guild meeting. Besides being one of our great writers he was also a wonderful speaker.

After the meeting he and I spoke for quite a while and somehow the conversation got around to neckties. We both hated wearing them.

I started to tell him that to that day, whenever I had put a tie on, I could almost feel my father --- He stopped me. And he finished my sentence: "You can feel your father standing behind you teaching you how to tie a knot in the tie. I feel it too," he said smiling, remembering.

We exchanged numbers and then in December I got this card from him, which hangs on the wall in my office to this day amongst many posters and pictures of my most memorable career highlights. It was Christmas wishes from Maggie and Ray Bradbury. And below the Christmas greetings was a poem Ray wrote that I'd like to share with you.

✷✷✷✷

Christmas Wishes from Maggie and Ray Bradbury

My father ties, I do not tie, my Christmas tie.
On some December night, long ago
I tried to try --
My first tie snarled upon my vest,
My hands all thumbs,
And presto-chango,
Something Awful This Way Comes.
My father quietly came by
And studied me and stood behind.
"Be blind," he said.
"Stay off mirrors.
Let your fingers
Learn to do."
His lesson lingers. What he said was true.
Eyes shut,
With him to help me over-up, around and under-out
Somehow a knot miraculous came about.
"There's nothing to it," said my Dad,
"Now, son, you do it. No, eyes *shut*!"
And with one last dear blind perceiving
He taught my crippled fingers
Arts of weaving. Then, turned away.
Well, to this day, how dare I boast,
I cannot do it.
I call that long-gone sweet-tobacco ghost
To help me through it.
He helps me yet;
Upon my neck, his breath, the scent of his last cigarette.
There is no death, for yestereve

His phantom fingers came and helped me tuck and weave.

If this be true (it *is*) he'll never die

My *father* ties, *I* do not tie, my Christmas tie.

It was simply signed: R.B. But underneath that he wrote out his signature.

As I said, on one wall in my office hang a collection of posters and photos, all fond memories. This poem is one of them.

Las Vegas

Paul Harris

AT ONE TIME I produced a TV series called 'The Magic Shop' for RKO Television. It was a variety show featuring the magic of top magicians and was syndicated throughout the country.

Our office was in the world famous Magic Castle, an old Victorian mansion on a hill above Hollywood with a winding driveway from the street to the entrance. While it was a private clubhouse for many magicians, guests could have dinner there and watch magicians perform in three showrooms as well as throughout the castle.

It was great for us. As a producer, I got to watch every act, meet every illusionist, and handpick my performers for every show.

✳✳✳✳

At our rehearsals I made the magicians do their illusions over and over telling them I was looking for the best camera angle. In truth I made them repeat their tricks time and time again because I was trying to figure out how they did what they did!

And no, I never did.

When the series ended, I was hired to be creative head of Transworld Productions out of Las Vegas.

When some of the magicians at the Magic Castle heard I was moving to Las Vegas they told me to go to a certain hotel every Wednesday night at midnight because it was where the Vegas magicians gathered to talk shop and to try out new close-up magic on each other and the few guests they allowed in.

✶✶✶✶

So, after moving to Nevada and settling in an apartment just off The Strip, come the first Wednesday I drove over to the hotel, found the meeting room, and met the magicians. Some lived in Las Vegas full-time, some were performing at different hotels, and some were just passing through.

There were about thirty magicians, I would guess, and a bunch of friends or tourists or local residents who came to watch these professionals ply their trade.

When I heard the great Dai Vernon was in the room I made my way over to his table where he was entertaining some people with his stories. There actually was a Dai Vernon Room at the Magic Castle, so prominent was he.

I introduced myself to him and told him I had produced 'The Magic Show' on TV. So he said he'd like to do a sleight-of-hand trick just for me.

Everyone gathered around. As Mr. Vernon opened a box to a new deck of cards, he told us that Winston Churchill had paid him a thousand dollars to teach him this trick.

He took the deck of cards, fanned them, and told me to take one card and not to show it to him but to everyone else and then return it to the deck. Doing so, he then returned the entire deck back into the box, closed it up, and placed the deck against the wall next to the table.

He told me to pick up the box, open it, and retrieve my card.

I picked up the box, opened it, and to everyone's astonishment, the deck of cards gone! But what was in the box was . . . my watch! Somehow he had taken it off my wrist, took the cards out (God knows where they were), and replaced the cards with my watch!

✳✳✳✳

At about two-thirty in the morning, way past my bedtime, I am so tired I can hardly keep my eyes open. It was fun talking to all the magicians and gratifying to know almost all of them had watched 'The Magic Show' regularly and were fans of the show.

As I'm contemplating leaving, a murmur begins to spread through the room.

"Paul Harris is coming!" "Paul Harris is coming!"

Obviously a famous magician was on his way in. I picture a Mandrake the Magician-type character wearing a tuxedo, a cape over his shoulders, a top hat, a pencil-thin mustache, a distinguished gentleman's gentleman.

In walks Paul Harris. He's a kid. Maybe twenty or twenty-one. He wore a stretched-out sweater and maybe scruffy blue jeans. Under his chin he carried a pile of books! He placed them on the table. Magicians waving money came running over and in minutes the pile of books was gone. Sold. Each and every one.

And with that Paul Harris was gone!

✳✳✳✳

I would have liked to have met this phenom but he was surrounded by the magicians and then, like a good illusionist, he disappeared! (Actually, he walked out the door.)

I find out about Paul Harris. He's an inventor. He invents magic tricks! Then he puts them down in a book. Then he sells his books. At the time I was told of the top ten magic books on the market --- seven were by Paul Harris.

One magic magazine called Paul "The most innovative magic mind of our day." Another magazine said, "Harris is one of the one hundred magicians who have shaped the art of magic in America."

I find out he also sells his tricks to the David Copperfields and the David Blaines of the world. Also he has been invited to Muslim countries, teaching magic to Sultanates and Shahs. For this he is paid a handsome fee.

A few days later I am at my new office at TransWorld Productions and I'm interviewing a bevy of young Las Vegas women, looking to hire a secretary.

One young lady comes into my office, introduces herself as Barbara Harris, and offhandedly I ask, "You related to Paul Harris, the magician?"

"He's my brother," she answers.

"You're hired! But only if you introduce me to Paul."

So that's how I got a secretary and that's how I met Paul Harris the magician.

✳✳✳✳

I've got to tell you about Paul's condo.

It was always midnight. He had these blackout drapes that were always closed over blackout window shades that were always drawn. For all I knew he might have had the windows painted too.

In the middle of the living room was a card table and a lamp. Otherwise complete blackness. And at this table he created, experimented, and improvised with a deck of cards or coins or pencils, sitting there alone for hours, night after night (there was no day in Paul's condo), using only his mind and his hands to conjure up close-up magic to astonish, surprise, and amaze.

Then, one day, he says to me, "I've got an idea for a movie."

"Oh?"

Paul starts: "A mother lives alone with her seventeen-year-old daughter. The girl is starting to get interested in guys. The mother's afraid she's going to lose her. So she tells the girl that they come from a strange parallel universe where everyone explodes when they try to make love."

I urge him to continue because so far he has my complete attention.

"Every time the girl goes out on a date, the mother secretly follows. And every time the girl and the date are about to kiss, a fire breaks out in a flowerpot right next to them, or if they're in a restaurant their food bursts into flames. All, of course, caused by the mother, who has set up the pyrotechnics beforehand."

"I love it," I laugh.

"Not only does the daughter believe she's got this combustible curse but she starts carrying around a fire extinguisher when she goes out on dates!"

What a stupidly original idea, I think to myself.

Paul finishes with, "Maybe you could help me with the rest of the story."

"Only if we can talk about it outside," I propose. "Working in the dark is good for magic but screenwriting requires light."

So, for the next couple of weeks, we sit in the pool at his condo and we finish the story.

And Paul sells it to a studio. And it gets made. You can look it up. 'Nice Girls Don't Explode' starring Barbara Harris (no relation to Paul), as the mother, Wallace Shawn as a friend, and Michelle Meyrink as the girl.

✳✳✳✳

That ended Paul's movie career. He went back to creating and teaching magic tricks, his first love. Tricks that magicians all over the world perform, amazing audiences, hearing their applause, getting their admiration, some going on to fame and fortune while Paul sits in the semi-darkness at his card table creating, experimenting, and improving his next batch of magic.

"Take a card. Any card . . ."

Barron Hilton

(reprinted from my book, 'The Perfect Pitch')

I'D BEEN THE creative head of Transworld Productions in Las Vegas for about six months at this point.

"You still living in Vegas?" It's my agent on the phone.

"Yep."

"The Las Vegas Hilton is looking for somebody to write a movie teaching people how to play the games of the casino; a movie that will run 24/7 in all the rooms in the hotel."

"Oh."

"Do you play blackjack?"

"Ah, no."

"Roulette."

"Uh-uh."

"Craps?"

"Looks too complicated."

"*Chemin de fer?*"

"Charmin de what?"

I could hear my agent slowly dying on the other end of the phone.

"Anyway," he mumbled, "I set up a meeting for you with all the

Hilton top brass, Thursday at 11. You'll be competing against about half a dozen writers. Good luck."

He hung up and I knew he was exasperated and felt I would be wasting my time.

****

When I have a pitch meeting I try to learn everything I can about the subject. First, I looked up 'gambling' in bookstores. There I learned the rules of all the games.

That's a start.

But every other writer is going to learn or know all the rules of the games, too. I needed something more. Something to dazzle the Hilton people.

But what?

I went to the Library at UNLV (University of Nevada at Las Vegas) where the librarian proudly told me that they possessed the largest collection of gambling books in America!

And so I started to read.

I found a book that went into great detail on the history of gambling. How each game started. That's it! That's my pitch! And maybe none of the other writers . . . I stopped myself. Forget the other writers. It's me and the Hilton execs and I've got to focus on them.

I knew my pitch was going to be long but I believed it was going to be damn interesting.

****

Thursday, come 11 o'clock and I'm sitting in an executive's suite in the Las Vegas Hilton with a group of guys in suits.

I started. "I want to tell, in this film, how every game started. For instance, let's start with dice. Anyone know the origins of dice?"

They all look from one to the other and either shrugged or shook their heads.

Inwardly I breathed a sigh of relief. *I am the authority figure in the room!*

"It started with cavemen." I'm off and running. "They would take the ankle bones of sheep and make markings on them. Then, with all the men gathered around, they would take turns throwing the ankle bones down on the ground to see who would gather wood for fire, who would hunt for food, who would kill the dinosaurs, and would take care of the women and children. Or something like that. But the ankle bones of sheep were the first dice!"

I looked around the room. They were all smiling.

I pulled out a deck of cards.

"No, no tricks," I told them. I held up the four kings. "Did you know these are portraits of four of the world's greatest rulers?"

More shrugs and headshaking.

"The King of Clubs, that's Alexander the Great. See, he holds an orb because he wanted to conquer the world.

"That's King David holding the harp on the King of Spades."

I'm rolling now.

"King of Hearts is Charlemagne and the King of Diamonds, Julius Caesar."

They were smiling again. Some were leaning forward in their chairs, a good sign.

"Now, talking about Caesar, he loved the chariot races. But what fascinated him the most was when a chariot would crash and turnover, the wheels would spin like crazy and cause all kinds of psychedelic colors within its whirling spokes.

"He was so fascinated with the spinning spokes, he had a 'wheel room' created in his palace. The wheel was placed on a stand and every time Caesar walked through the room a man guarding the wheel would spin it for Caesar's enjoyment.

"Well, the story goes that four families were preparing for battle over a piece of land. Each claimed to be the rightful owner.

"Caesar came up with an idea. He positioned the heads of the four families around the wheel and made a marking on the rim. He then had the wheel spun and said, 'Wherever the marking stops, that family will be the sole and legal owner.'

"Caesar was so enchanted with the suspense of where that marking would stop that he decided to make it three-out-of-five! (Okay, I made that part up!) But that, gentlemen," I concluded, "was the beginning of the roulette wheel!"

More smiles, more nods.

Now here's where I threw in the kicker.

"As I see it, by showing how these games started, it legitimizes the word 'gambling' and to the neophyte it's almost like giving them permission to gamble. After all, cavemen did it, Caesar did it, French kings did it."

They had the idea of what I was planning to do and I felt all I could do at that point was screw it up.

But I continued, "Talk about French kings, Chemin de fer was created by a French king who thought it would be a good way to teach his children mathematics. He---"

"Enough, Mr. Rotcop." Barron Hilton stopped me. "I think we are all in agreement. You have overwhelmed us with your knowledge. The job is yours."

And that's how I got to write the gambling movie that played at Hilton Hotels in Vegas, Reno, and who-knows-where 24/7, teaching people to play the games of the casino.

And to this day I've never bellied up to a gambling table.

When I called my agent to tell him that I got the assignment, there was a long pause on the other end.

I think he fainted!

Frankie Carr

FRANKIE CARR WAS an entertainer in Las Vegas and he'd been there for many, many years. He was a short guy, kind of reminded me of Mickey Rooney. He played the lounges of all the hotels in Las Vegas with his group of musicians, 'The Novelites.'

Somehow he and I became friends. When I would go to see his show he would always introduce me to the audience in the middle of the act. "... And here in our audience from Hollywood, here to do research on me because I'll be starring in his next movie, producer and writer Ken Rotcop."

And he'd make me stand, and the spotlight went on me, and the audience would applaud. Of course there was no movie and I had no idea what he was talking about. But it was a lot of fun.

****

One day while working for TransWorld Productions in Las Vegas, my boss came into my office. There was a director who wanted to talk to me about writing a commercial.

I met with the director and she said, "I've been hired to do a commercial for Gus Gallo's Crazy Horse Saloon. Do you know about Gus Gallo and the Crazy Horse Saloon?"

"No."

She said, "It's on Flamingo and Paradise. It's kind of a strip joint but it's where all waitresses stand on the top of this circular bar and when you order a drink, the girls lean over and pop the bottle top of your beer while you look down their low-cut blouses. If you're interested in writing the commercial you need to talk to Tony Albanese, he runs the place," and she handed me his card.

Well I called Tony Albanese and he said, "Meet me at the coffee shop at the Riviera Hotel tomorrow and we'll talk business." So I met him in the coffee shop.

Tony Albanese, I would say, was in his mid-30s. He was a swarthy good-looking Italian guy. He wore his shirts down to his navel and he had all these gold chains around his neck. He proceeded to tell me that he wanted to do a commercial for Gus Gallo, his boss, for the Crazy Horse Salon. "Do you have any ideas?"

So I said, "Yeah, I'd like to do something with Frankie Carr. Frankie Carr's such a cute looking lovable guy and I'm told he's the opposite of the kind of clientele that you get at the Crazy Horse." (Meaning all of the mob types that came there.)

So he said, "Yeah, we like Frankie. Come up with a script and make sure it better be good." So I did and he decided to hire me to write the commercial.

I came up with three different skits that Frankie Carr would do in the one minute commercial.

One where he's smothered with dancing women, they're all over him and his head pops up and he says, "This is fun but I'd rather be at Gus Gallo's Crazy Horse Saloon."

And another time where he is playing golf and he sinks a long putt and he says, "You think that's exciting? You want to see exciting? Go over to Gus Gallo's Crazy Horse Saloon."

And then the third one was Frankie on an inflatable lounge raft in a swimming pool and a girl would leap on him drowning him and he would pop up spitting out water and saying, "Nobody drinks pool water at Gus Gallo's Crazy Horse Saloon!"

Everybody loved the script and we shot the commercial.

∗∗∗∗

My deal with Tony Albanese was that I would get half of the money up front and half the money when the commercial was done. I got the up-front money and when we finished shooting and editing the commercial we went to the Crazy Horse Saloon to show it to Albanese and all the waitresses. It was during the day, quiet, and everybody was excited to see the commercial.

We ran the commercial and Albanese, the girls, and a few drunks at the bar applauded. They laughed in all the right places and when it was over everybody shouted, "Show it again. Show it again." So we showed it a second time and a third time.

Then I walked into Tony Albanese's office. I said, "Are you happy with it, Tony?"

"Yeah."

I asked, "Can I have my check for the other half now that it's complete?"

"Forget it. I gave you enough money."

"Tony, we had a deal. You only paid me half the money."

"You ain't getting more money. Whatever I gave you is enough."

I walked out. I knew that Gus Gallo was a big mob boss in Las Vegas. I knew enough not to have an argument with Tony.

∗∗∗∗

So I called Frankie Carr. "Frankie, let me tell you what happened today."

I told him the story and he said, "I'll get back to you."

He called me a couple days later. "We got an appointment tomorrow morning."

He gave me an address. "Be there at nine o'clock in the morning. Not nine o'five and not eight fifty-five. You be there at exactly 9 o'clock."

So the next day I go to this beautiful house in the Beverly Hills section of Las Vegas and ring the doorbell at exactly nine. I'm ushered into the house and I meet this very tall, very distinguished looking, gray-haired older man. Let's call him Mr. B.

Mr. B looks me over then asks Frankie, "What's going on? What happened?"

By this time the commercial is playing on every station in Las Vegas and playing day and night.

Frankie tells Mr. B that I made this commercial and that Tony Albanese stiffed me out of half my fee.

Mr. B looks at me and smiles. "You made that commercial? I love that commercial. I *really* love that commercial. That Tony Albanese, he's getting a little out of hand. He's *really* getting a little out of hand."

Mr. B shakes his head sadly and sighs. Then to me he says, "Sue him."

"But sir, I don't know if you know but he works for Gus Gallo and I hear these people are like mob people. I can't sue him."

"Don't worry about a thing. Sue him."

And as I'm talking to him, Frankie Carr is standing behind this guy and with his finger, he's pushing his nose to one side, and pointing at the guy and I don't know what the hell that means until we get outside and Frankie says, "You know I was giving you the sign. This is the mob, the Mafia, and this guy is the Don. You're talking to the Don and you're telling him that Gus Gallo is in the mob? Are you nuts?"

I say, "I didn't know." And I didn't know that pushing the nose to the side indicated a broken nose, which, evidently, all mobsters have.

"Now you gotta sue Tony Albanese. You got an order from the Don!"

****

Well by this time I'd been working for TransWorld for about two years but when I got a job offer to come back to Los Angeles I went back. I filed suit and I got a letter from the court giving me a date to show up in Las Vegas to sue not Tony Albanese but Gus Gallo. Oh boy. So I called my friend Jerry Siegel, who was the tallest friend that I had. He's about 6'3".

I said, "Jerry, we're going to Las Vegas next week and I want you to come as my guest and all I want you to do is stand tall, don't slouch, and stand next to me." So Jerry came to Vegas with me.

****

We were the first case called out of the docket. "J. Kenneth Rotcop versus Gus Gallo's Crazy Horse Saloon."

I got up to the bench and I saw, for the first time, this husky, middle-aged man who could play linebacker for the Green Bay Packers. Gus Gallo. He went up to the judge. The judge turned away from me and said to Gus, "What time do we tee off today, Gus?"

Gus said, "Two-fifteen."

The judge said. "Okay, I'll see you there. Now what's going on?"

And I'm saying to myself, *He's teeing off with this guy at two-fifteen? No way am I going to win this case. Let alone get my money.*

So, I told the judge the story and he said to me, "You made that commercial? I love that commercial! I love that commercial!" He turned to Gus and said, "Pay the man, Gus! Pay the man!"

So Gus Gallo turned to me and said, "Come to my office, I'll have a check for you."

Gus, with his entourage, started to walk out and I was behind them with my friend Jerry standing next to me and all of a sudden I felt a heavy hand on my shoulder and I think I hit the roof! I didn't know who the heck it was.

I turned around and it was a Marshall, and the Marshall said, "You don't go to his office to collect the check. We'll go, we'll collect the check for you. You'll wait in our office and when I hand the check to you, you get in your car, go to the airport, and you get the hell out of town." And, he did. The Marshall got the check, gave it to us, and we went directly to the airport, got on a plane, and got the hell out of Las Vegas.

✳✳✳✳

But that wasn't the end of the story. About two weeks later my closest friend in Las Vegas, named Marty Mendelson, called.

"Well, you did it this time, Rotcop."

I said, "Did what?"

"They found Tony Albanese out in the desert with two bullets in the back of his head."

"Jeez," I swallowed my breath. "Marty, it had nothing to do with me."

It turned out that Tony Albanese was trying to buy the Jolly Trolley, which is just across the street from the Sahara Hotel, without including the 'family,' the other members of the mafia. And they didn't like that he was going behind their backs and trying to buy something on his own. So they taught him a lesson.

✳✳✳✳

How do I know? Because, Hank Greenspun, the editor of the Las Vegas Sun and I were at a dinner and I happened to mention to him, "You know every time there is a mob killing in Las Vegas, it's like on the front page one day and the next day you don't even read about it."

He said, "Yeah, because the mob takes care of their own. Whenever they want to do somebody in, they take him out to the desert, they put two bullets in the back of the neck, one bullet on top of the other. It's their way of the telling the police not to worry about it, they've taken care of 'family' business.

"They also do it for suicides in Las Vegas. If a chambermaid walks into a room and sees that somebody has hanged himself or overdosed or slit his wrists because he's lost all of his money gambling, the maids have a phone number to call. The mob sends over two guys with white coats. They take the body out the back way, they take it out to the desert, two bullets in the back of the neck, and report it as a gangland killing because nobody commits suicide in Las Vegas. Mob killings are acceptable. Suicides aren't."

Funny thing about the Jolly Trolley. I used to eat there all the time. They served the best prime rib in Las Vegas. At that time I think it was two ninety-five for a three course dinner. You couldn't beat the food or the price.

In the back room of the Jolly Trolley, separated by a curtain from the restaurant, were all these strippers. I'd finish eating dinner and I'd watch for a couple minutes and then I would go on my merry way.

✳✳✳✳

Here's a story about the Jolly Trolley. First I have to tell you about a tennis tournament in Las Vegas that I signed up for. It was a pro-amateur tournament and they had these pros come in from all over the country. Not the big-name pros but teaching pros from the different clubs throughout the United States.

And the amateurs were given a pro to play with and the pro that I was given was from Baltimore, Maryland. His name was Noah Hirsch and I went to the airport to pick him up. He and his wife got off the plane and the first thing out of his mouth was, "How fast can we get on the tennis court?"

He was anxious to see whether his partner was any good at all and within an hour we were at the Tropicana. They had indoor courts in those days. We were at the Trop hitting tennis balls and to make a long story short, we won the tournament. That was great.

✳✳✳✳

As much as Noah liked being in Vegas his wife liked it more. She fell in love with the place and she decided that she wanted to move there. And so Noah who was just starting law school, literally quit his job in Baltimore, gave up the tennis club that he was a pro at, and moved to Las Vegas to see if he could get work there and go to law school at UNLV.

She got work before him. She got a job as a stripper in the back room of the Jolly Trolley. From that moment on I never went in again. I was always afraid that she'd see me peeking through the curtain.

✳✳✳✳

Tony Albanese, Gus Gallo, Noah's wife, the Don and the Judge . . . what a time it was! I miss Frankie Carr and Marty Mendelson, two dear friends, and I must confess, I miss the two ninety-five prime rib dinners at the Jolly Trolley.

Bill Kaysing

BILL BUTTERS CAME into my office one day. He was president of TransWorld Productions in Las Vegas. I was creative head.

"Ever hear of a guy named Bill Kaysing?" he asked.

"Uh, uh."

"He's called 'The Father of the Great Moon Hoax.'"

I shrugged. "Who's the mother?"

Butters didn't think that was funny. "He may be a crackpot or . . . anyway, he's written a book called 'What Never Went To The Moon.'"

"Can't say I've read it."

Butters had a way of talking right through what anybody else was saying. "You know the guys who walked on the moon? According to Kaysing it never happened.

"He says the whole thing was shot out there in the Nevada desert."

He nodded southeast of my office somewhere. "Maybe eighty, ninety miles from here."

"I've heard those theories," I quickly threw in.

"Well," plows in Butters, "Kaysing is living in a trailer here in Vegas and I bought the rights to his book. I want you to work with him and write a script."

"But everybody knows we really did go to the moon. Who's going to go see a movie about---"

"Read the book first. Then meet the guy. Come up with an angle that'll make it all palatable. Here's his number. Put down that sports magazine you're reading and call him."

✳✳✳✳

I called Kaysing. I read his book. Turned out he was head of technical publications for Rocketdyne, the company that made the rocket engines for the space program. From 1958 to 1962 Kaysing was privy to documents pertaining to, among other things, the Apollo space program. In his book he argued that one did not need to be a scientist or engineer to determine that a hoax was being perpetrated.

When he saw that everyone in the company was going along with the fabrication, he quit Rocketdyne and followed the Apollo 'myth' closely to where he felt confident enough to write his book.

Of course all the conspiracy fanatics gobbled up every copy of 'We Never Went To The Moon' and worshipped at Bill Kaysing's hiking boots.

✳✳✳✳

So Kaysing and I went out for a cup of mineral water. We talked for hours.

He was a pleasant man, tall and slim with a quiet way about him. It seems all his other books were about recognizing and naming trees and plants and flowers and taking nature hikes into the wilderness.

He made me look at a piece of animated film made by NASA that showed what it would be like when the capsule landed on the moon. The thrust of the flames that shot out at the bottom would cause a huge crater in the ground.

But when he showed me footage of the actual moon landing, there was hardly a divot under the capsule.

"They goofed," he smiled.

He then told me that the Apollo would have enough fuel to get up to the moon but in no way did it have enough to get back to Earth.

Of course, all of this stuff was in Bill's book. But he was just getting started. He had theories, he had circumstantial evidence, he had suppositions. He showed me photos that had been photoshopped (only they didn't use that expression back then).

"Lies, lies, and more lies." All covered up, according to Kaysing, by the government, NASA, the FBI, and, of course, Rocketdyne and anyone else who made components for the space program.

And, he added, anyone who was willing to come forth and tell the truth . . . died mysteriously.

✳✳✳✳

And then there was the story about the astronauts who had come to the Nevada desert to practice for the actual first moon landing.

The astronauts were put in one of the luxurious Vegas hotels on the Strip. Every morning they were picked up and taken out to the desert, eighty or ninety miles away, where they would simulate the moon landing at a highly secretive army installation.

You've seen the picture of the capsule with four legs. Well, they'd get in the practice capsule, were hoisted way up in the air, and would be dropped to simulate a moon landing. The astronauts were controlling the speed and direction of the landing.

They did it over and over. Good practice. Except, according to Kaysing, they didn't, *not even once*, land standing up! On every practice landing, the capsule hit the ground and rolled over on its side!

There's more to Kaysing's story. In the evenings, back in the luxury hotel, they were wined and dined by Las Vegas bigwigs. They were also accompanied by some of the Strip's prettiest 'showgirls' to keep them company.

So, come morning, with our astronauts hung over, off to the desert they'd go for more practice moon landings, giggling or sleeping it off in the van.

At least according to Bill Kaysing.

Finally, NASA decided to get them the hell out of Vegas and shipped them off to Houston where they could keep an eye on the musketeers.

NASA put them in front of huge television sets like you would find in an amusement park arcade. Instead of racing cars, they simulated moon landings. On the TV, the capsule never fell over!

That, according to Bill Kaysing, is how they got their experience landing on the moon. If, in fact, they ever truly went.

****

Bill and I spent many days together. He talked, I listened. He told me what his life has been like since leaving Rocketdyne and writing his infamous book. Sure, there were the admirers, the conspiracy fanatics who carried Bill's book around with them like it was a bible titled 'The Gospel According to Kaysing'. But mostly there were the righteous ones, the ones who ostracized Kaysing, and ridiculed him, and badgered him, and, yes, bullied him.

He claimed that wherever he and his wife Ruth put down their trailer there were always men within thirty, forty feet just standing around watching them, watching the trailer, watching where they walked, watching where they shopped.

I don't know if I believed Bill or not but I knew I found the angle for the script. It wasn't about Bill's accusations in the book, it was about what happened to *the man and his wife for writing the book.*

You see, right or wrong, Bill really believed everything he wrote about and everything he told me. These were his opinions. His conclusions. Interesting? Credible? You don't have to agree with him. But he certainly was not a stupid man. Nor was he belligerent.

He was a man who wrote books on plants and flowers and trees; things that grow in the earth. And he truly believed we never went to the moon.

✴✴✴✴

I wrote the script based on what Bill and Ruth had gone through. I wrote about the astronauts who had died when their Apollo 1 burst into flames and they were locked in and couldn't get out. Bill claimed they were about to tell the truth about the program.

I wrote about the mysterious death of a safety inspector whose car was hit by a train and he was killed after he had testified before the United States Congress and the disappearance of his 500-page report on the Apollo 1 fire.

I wrote about the astronauts partying in Las Vegas and the fiasco of the moon landing exercises.

But mostly I wrote about Bill and Ruth. Don Quixote fighting windmills. Like my boss, Bill Butters had said, "Maybe the guy's nuts. Maybe he's not."

We sold the script to J. Arthur Rank, a major London studio at the time. They couldn't raise the moon to make the movie. Maybe the story was too controversial. Maybe the script wasn't any good. Whatever.

But take a walk with Bill Kaysing up in the wilds of Mount Charleston above the city of Las Vegas and watch him name and tell you about every plant, every tree, every flower.

The man knew his flora.

Back To Holly-wood

Allison Hayes & Jack Klugman

YOU REMEMBER AN actress named Allison Hayes?

Probably not. I didn't. She went from being Miss Washington, D.C. in the 1949 Miss America Pageant to playing in a zillion low-budget B movies in the 1950's like: 'Sign Of The Pagan,' 'The Unearthly,' 'The Disembodied,' 'The Undead,' 'The Zombies Of Mora Tau,' 'The Hypnotic Eye,' 'The Crawling Hand,' (these are real titles, honest) and the one she is best known for, the cult classic, 'Attack Of The 50-Foot Woman.'

That was Allison, the 50-Foot Woman.

Somehow I had missed seeing all of them.

But a friend of mine knew her. And she came to the conclusion that I should write a screenplay based on Allison's life.

This is the story she told me:

After being the 50-Foot Woman, in 1957, Allison had a hard time getting better roles. Finally, in 1963 she played a continuous role in the soap opera 'General Hospital.'

But she began experiencing health problems. It was hard for her to work. She began walking with a cane and was in constant severe pain.

She went from doctor to doctor. None of them could correctly diagnose her problem.

Her strength deteriorated. She thought about suicide.

One symptom she kept telling the doctors about was that she felt ants crawling over the bridge of her nose.

The doctors thought Allison was losing it, or in fact, had lost it. At best they thought she was a hypochondriac.

She decided to do research on her own.

She made her way to the library at the UCLA Medical School.

By this time she was so weak, she crawled through the stacks. She would sit on the floor and knock books off of the shelves using her cane so that they would fall on the floor and she could read them.

Hours of futility went by until she found a medical book that talked about the metal poisoning of factory workers.

The one symptom they all had in common was the sensation of feeling ants crawling over the bridge of their nose!

Now an invalid, Allison hired a toxicologist to test a calcium health product she had been taking regularly for a number of years.

Sure enough, this so-called health product was filled with lead.

The calcium supplement was made of bone meal from ground-up bones of cows. Cows that probably were grazing next to the highways. Cars were spewing out toxic fumes, which, like rain falling from the skies, fell onto the grass that the cows ate. Grass that was toxic --- contaminated with lead from the gas fumes.

The lead got into the cows' bones. When the cows were slaughtered their bones were ground-up and sold as a calcium supplement.

Allison Hayes took this supplement every day for years. The idea was to make her bones, teeth, and nails stronger.

But what Allison did was, she poisoned herself.

She became a one-woman advocate to abolish toxic bone meal.

Almost single-handedly she was responsible for getting the FDA to ban bone meal for human consumption. It was her most distinguished role.

Not too long after that, Allison was diagnosed with Leukemia, her health deteriorated to the point that she was hardly recognizable, and just days before her forty-seventh birthday, the 50-Foot Woman had died.

That was the story my friend told me.

All I could say was, "Wow."

"She had two close friends in the Hollywood community. Raymond Burr and Jack Klugman."

"This would be perfect for Klugman," I said.

****

Jack Klugman was starring in a dramatic series at the time called 'Quincy, M.E.' in which he played a coroner who investigates suspicious deaths.

So a meeting was set up. Klugman of course remembered Allison, liked the idea behind the script, and a deal was made.

Allison Hayes would live again through 'Quincy, M.E.'

A couple of weeks later, a meeting was set for lunch at the studio for me to give Klugman an update on what I was writing. We were to meet in his trailer. I told my friend that I was to talk to Klugman about the project over lunch.

I was wrong. When I arrived at his trailer he sat at a table eating; I stood and watched him. I turned on my tape recorder. We discussed the story and he briefly reminisced about Allison. When I started to tell him about one particular scene I had already written, he got very excited.

"No, no, no. That's wrong. Here's how that scene should go!" And, very excitedly, he began to play out the scene, acting out every character, hands waving (fork still in right hand) and, in his excitement, he was spitting out bits of food on my shirt.

Now, remember I had tape-recorded the entire meeting. I learned years earlier never to attend a meeting without recording it, because I'm apt to forget something important one minute after the meeting is over.

When lunch ended, Klugman said we'd meet again tomorrow "over lunch" and go over the changes.

The next day, same thing. He was eating, I was standing. I wanted a bib but I thought it might have been in bad taste.

He read the scene that I had rewritten verbatim and he shook his head, put the pages down, and announced, "This is shit!"

"But it's just as you gave me." I nodded toward my tape recorder sitting on the edge of his table. "It's exactly word for word. It's on the tape. Do you want to hear it?"

"I don't give a shit what's on the tape, I never said these words."

With food hurling from his mouth onto my second shirt, I tried to talk calmly.

My position was he was entitled to hate the scene but to at least admit he had said it, or at least listen to the tape.

His position was I was a lousy writer.

By the time I got home from our 'lunch' I was informed by my agent that I was fired off of the project.

Allison Hayes' story never got made.

✳✳✳✳

She may have made only B movies, but her major accomplishment was getting toxic bone meal banned. God knows how many lives she saved, at the price of her own. I'm just sorry that episode of 'Quincy' was never made. She would have used the credit.

Remy O'Neill

REMY O'NEILL IS a Hollywood actress. Never heard of her? Then you haven't seen 'Hollywood Hot Tubes 1 and 2'. Or 'Return To Horror High'. Or some of the psycho-thrillers or other soft porn movies that she's been in.

She's worked pretty steadily. Small parts, bit parts, nude parts, crazy ladies, nice ladies, fun loving ladies, demonic ladies. Don't laugh! Maybe this isn't mainstream Hollywood but she's worked. She's acted. She's made movies. And maybe she's even made a living.

✳✳✳✳

But we're getting ahead of our story. It actually started with my sister, who fell in love with an Israeli, Ronnie Lapin, who had come to our country to attend an American college. They married and my father paid for him to go on to medical school at the University of Indiana.

Everything was idyllic in the marriage until they decided to move out to the west coast where Ronnie started a practice in Orange County.

One day he announced to my sister, his wife, that he was leaving her because he was having an affair with his nurse and they were going to get married.

And so he divorced my sister and married his nurse. I honestly have forgotten her real name.

****

Now, I was living in Las Vegas working at TransWorld Productions when I got a call from Arnold Shapiro, a producer in Los Angeles. He had sold his first TV series. It was to be a reality show with a therapist who would deal with couples whose relationships were in turmoil.

A half hour daily show and the title was, oddly enough, 'Couples.' Every day the therapist would deal with a different couple, either married or going together, who were anxious to keep their relationship from falling apart.

Arnold asked me to come back to L.A. and produce the pilot for him and so I took a leave of absence from TransWorld Productions.

****

There were two therapists Arnold was considering. He said we would actually make three pilots with each of them and then pick out the therapist we were going to use and the best of the pilots to show the network.

The two therapists were Dr. Walter Brackelmanns, new to television, and Dr. Joyce Brothers, a famed radio therapist with a huge following.

My first day on the job I told Arnold of my concern: "Who is going to want to come on television and tell all America about the problems they're having? I mean, we might get one but getting both parties I think is going to be next to impossible. I certainly don't know anyone who would do it."

Arnold said they had put an ad in the L.A. Times looking for couples whose relationships are in trouble to audition for a reality show. They were to show up at the studio the next day.

As I drove to the studio the next morning there were *hundreds* of couples, lined up on the sidewalk. The line went around the block! The guard at the gate was going crazy. And I was giggling like a kid who found a puppy under the Christmas tree!

We started picking couples. And as we did I remembered a conversation I had had with my ex-brother-in-law who was now a huge success in his medical practice and had recently bought a *castle* on a hilltop somewhere in Orange County. I remembered him telling me about his wife, the now retired nurse, wanting to be an actress and asking me if I could help her out.

So I called him. I told him I was producing a pilot. I told him what it was about and that if he and his wife would come on the show it would be a good piece of tape that she could use to show other producers. I told him to make up any ol' problem so there was conflict and the therapist would then give them tips to live by.

So Ronnie, wanting to help get his wife's career going, committed for both of them, and the day of the taping they were there bright and early. They were one of the couples that were on one of Dr. Walter Brackelmanns' three pilots.

****

The show started, and Ronnie's wife turned to him and blurted out, "Ron, I'm going to say something to you that I would be afraid to say if we were in private because I'm afraid it would go badly. I want a divorce. I really want out of this marriage. It's not working. We've become strangers and I'm afraid of you when you come home from the office or the hospital and I'm always afraid you're going to do something to me."

In the control booth Arnold turned to me. "They're great! Did you rehearse them?"

I shook my head. I didn't know if Ronnie and his wife had made up this great scenario or if she really wanted a divorce! I'm thinking either this is legit or she is one hell of an actress!

It went on. Ronnie was playing the flabbergasted husband. She had all the lines, like how he needed to attend anger management classes; how he would be nice to his patients but cold and menacing to her. And stuff like that.

When Dr. Brackelmanns started to give them advice, tears ran down her cheeks just like in the movies! Or were they real?! I hadn't a clue.

The show ended. I went over to them. I didn't know whether to congratulate them for a great performance or extend my apologies.

To make a long story short, her performance sold the show to the network. I finished my job and went back to Las Vegas. And Ronnie and his wife got divorced.

Everything she talked about on the show, everything she accused him of was her true feelings. She said if it wasn't for 'Couples' she might not have ever gotten the nerve to leave him. Ronnie couldn't believe what was happening. (And my sister got her revenge!)

****

Months went by and I received an invitation to a party in Hollywood. It was from Ronnie's second ex-wife, the nurse trying to turn actress.

I happened to be in town that weekend so someone fixed me up with a date and we went to the party. My date's name was Remy O'Neill. She and Ronnie's ex-wife hit it off. They became fast friends, at least for the night.

The next day I got a call from Ronnie's ex-wife. "Do you remember your date's name from last night?" she asked.

"Yeah, why?"

"Because I'm stealing her name. I love the name. From now on *I'm* Remy O'Neill."

"Does the *real* Remy O'Neill know?" I asked.

I'll never forget her answer. "From now on I'm the *real* Remy O'Neill!"

"Okay. Whatever," I shrugged. We said our goodbyes and hung up.

After that, I got busy with my writing. She broke into the soft porn movie industry and we never kept in touch. I never saw any of her movies.

Thanks to Remy, the second real Remy, Arnold Shapiro's show 'Couples' ran two, maybe three years. I never again saw or spoke to the first Remy. Don't know what happened to her.

Dr. Ronnie Lapin married a third time. I hear she was a Miss Israel. A few years later I was told he overdosed on drugs and died.

Arnold Shapiro produced other shows. Dr. Walter Brackelmanns went back to his practice.

$$****$$

And the second real Remy O'Neill? I guess she still keeps going out on auditions, still does showcases, and probably still goes to casting calls. But, according to her credits that I picked off the computer she is still working.

Funny how things work out.

Gerry Fried

GERRY FRIED IS one of Hollywood's most successful composers. He presently lives in Santa Fe, where he is in residence with the Santa Fe Symphony. Before that he composed music for many, many feature films and television shows. He is probably best known for doing the music for 'Roots,' a groundbreaking miniseries about Black-American history. He also did the music for Stanley Kubrick's films. And he composed the score for my movie, 'For Us, The Living: The Story Of Medgar Evers.'

****

Gerry was married to Annabelle and they had a son, whose name was Zack. When Zack was four years old he was feeling sick, so they took him to the doctor and the doctor discovered that he had some kind of illness that required him to have numerous blood transfusions. His growth was stunted, he was a little guy, but when he was feeling well Gerry would bring him down to the tennis court and I would roll a ball to him and he would stop it with a giggle and throw the ball back to me. He was just a cute, cheerful kid.

Finally the doctors said that they were done with the blood transfusions, that he was fine and was going to live a long healthy life.

But a number of months later he got sick again and went back to the hospital. They ran tests on him and came back with the news that Zack had AIDS and was not going to make it. Evidently one of the blood transfusions was tainted. And within six months Zack was dead.

****

Gerry turned to Annabelle a few weeks after and said, "I think we should have another child right away."

And Annabelle said, "Are you crazy?! I feel Zack in every room in this house! I *feel* him, Gerry. How can you talk that way? I'm in mourning. I'm grieving. I can't even have you touch me, let alone think of having another child!"

And Gerry said, "We're not getting any younger, Annabelle. *I'm* not getting any younger. If Zack were here, I know he would approve."

"I don't care," and the argument went on and on to the point where they soon separated. They had Zack cremated and Gerry kept half the ashes and Annabelle kept the other half.

****

Annabelle, who worked as a seamstress making costumes for movies, was kind of a quiet, shy lady. She got the courage to travel to Washington, D.C. and spoke to Congress, where she testified before Congress about all the people of all ages who were dying of AIDS. She suggested doing a memorial to them. She said, "What I suggest is we make a patch quilt, with each square dedicated to someone who has died of AIDS. I want to let all America know about the AIDS epidemic. Each patch, different than the others, would be made by a loved one left behind."

Within months, the patches came in by the thousands. If you ever remember seeing a picture of it on the lawn in front of the Washington

Monument, it was huge. It was about two football fields long and wide. All patches with names of people who had already died. One of the patches had Zack's name on it.

****

Zack used to love to go out to the Griffith Park in Los Angeles, where they had a permanent train exhibit. They also had a choo-choo train for kids. The choo-choo would go around the park and there were a lot of locomotives for kids to climb into and run around in. Zack would love to go and Gerry and Annabelle, when they were married, would take Zack out every weekend to Griffith Park to ride on the choo-choo train.

And when Zack died and a year went by and it was the anniversary of his death, Gerry decided to go out to Griffith Park, at nine o'clock at night when the park would be closed, and spread Zack's ashes on the railroad tracks; since that's what his young son would've liked.

When he arrived it was quiet and dark and the only light came from the moon. He took his ashes and started to spread them on the flowers that surrounded the railroad track, when he heard somebody coming and thought, *Oh sure, now I'm going to be thrown out.*

It was Annabelle. She'd come to spread *her* ashes. They hadn't seen each other since the breakup.

They smiled awkwardly, relieved to see each other.

They spread their ashes. Tears welling in their eyes. And as they walked out of the park, Gerry took Annabelle's hand. He walked her to her car, she got in, and they went their separate ways.

Carl Winderl

I HAD JUST finished my lecture on a cruise ship. Some of the audience came up to me to talk and ask questions. After the group thinned out, a good-looking couple introduced themselves. He was Carl Winderl and his wife was Ronda. Carl taught in the English Department at a Nazarene University and Ronda was the head of the Drama Department.

They said, because they enjoyed listening to me, they were sending me a chapbook, a long poem that Carl had written that had won a number of Christian book awards.

The poem was the story of the Immaculate Conception told through the eyes of Mary. It was beautiful and supposedly the first time that a poem had been written from Mary's point of view about the birth and the life of Jesus.

I contacted Carl and I told him how much I enjoyed the poem, and he said, "I have a manuscript that I just finished and I would love to send it to you. I would love for you to edit it. It's quite long but I think you'll really enjoy it."

"Is it a religious story like your poem?"

Carl said, "No, nothing like it at all."

"Fine, send it on to me."

****

So I got this manuscript, in two boxes, and I started to read. And I laughed and it was funny and it was cute and it was charming and all of the characters were great. It was about as far removed from Jesus, Mary, and the Immaculate Conception as you can imagine. What a surprise!

The story was about a man in his 40s, who was a schoolteacher, who was single, had divorced his wife, and was looking for something to do with his life. He played, I think, the guitar and he thought, *Wouldn't it be nice if I could hook up with a band.*

So he started to look through the newspapers in the ad column, and sure enough there was an ad that read, "Would you like to join a garage band? We meet every afternoon at four o'clock." And it gave the address. "If you're interested come on by."

The following afternoon this man got in his car and drove to the address. He went to the back of the house with his guitar because he heard music coming from the garage and he saw four high school kids all playing musical instruments, and here he was, a man in his 40s.

And he kind of apologized and said, "I was hoping you were . . ." And they said, "Yeah we were hoping you were too . . ." He started to walk away and one of the boys said, "You're already here, why don't you sit in with us." So he did.

He played the guitar and they liked it. It added a nice blend to the instruments they had and they said, "Maybe you can go on a gig with us."

"I don't know . . . maybe . . . well, maybe it'll be unique, one old man and four kids. Sure. Let me know when you get a gig."

Well the gigs they lined up were afternoon birthday parties for five-year-olds, four-year-olds, three-year-olds, all in the neighborhood. And wherever the band went, the man would go with them.

And who was there with the kids? The mothers. While the kids were eating ice cream and cake, he would start to talk to the mothers. He was a good-looking man, he was single, they felt sorry for him, and one time after another, wherever the party was for these young kids, some mother would take him by the hand and take him up to one of the bedrooms for adult entertainment. And he started to enjoy the garage band even more.

✳✳✳✳

And that was about as far as I got into the manuscript, about fifty or sixty pages or so, when I got a phone call from Ronda, Carl's wife, who said, "Mr. Rotcop, I understand you have Carl's manuscript."

"I do."

She said, "Will you please send it back immediately."

"Why?"

I could hear she was getting upset. "We belong to a Nazarene University. If word ever gets out about Carl's manuscript, he'll be fired. Please send it back immediately."

"But, it's fiction," I argued.

"It's trash! Carl writes Christian biblical poetry, not that . . . that pulp."

"It's not pulp. It's very good. Well written, humorous, sexy." Oops. I should never have said *sexy*.

"Just send it back and promise me you will not tell Carl of this conversation. As far as he's concerned we never talked. Promise?" She waited for my response.

I thought of something clever to say. Nothing clever came out.

"I promise."

And with that she hung up.

He was such a good writer. With a very commercial voice. If I had finished the story, and if it held up, I not only could get it published but I wouldn't have been surprised if it became a bestseller! It was unique and refreshing and a very fast read. I could even see the possibilities of a movie.

I sent the manuscript back. No letter. No explanation. Just two boxes filled with all the typewritten pages.

＊＊＊＊

I didn't hear from Carl for about four years. One day I got a postcard from his publisher announcing another religious chapbook.

So I emailed Carl and asked if anything had ever happened with his manuscript.

I didn't hear back from him. I heard from Ronda.

Her email simply read: "Don't ever use this email again."

＊＊＊＊

Sorry Carl.

Sister Janet

I WAS LISTENING to the radio one morning and heard Michael Jackson (not the singer but a talk show host) interviewing Sister Janet.

It seemed she lived in the barrio of East Los Angeles and ran with the gangs that were constantly killing each other (and innocents). She evidently stopped more killings, more gang wars, more ugly confrontations then the entire Los Angeles Police Department in those neighborhoods.

Her story sounded special and exciting. *Maybe there's a television movie in it*, I thought. I already had this Sister Janet cast in my head. Angela Lansbury would be perfect as the kindly middle-aged nun who was beloved and protected by the gangs on the streets of East L.A.

I called the radio station, told them I wanted to speak to Sister Janet, and they took my number and said if she was interested she would call me.

The very next day she called. She was interested.

We set up a meeting at my co-writer's apartment in Beverly Hills for the following afternoon.

****

I expected a white-haired, middle-aged lady dressed in a black habit.

The doorbell rang. I answered the door. And there stood what could have been Julie Andrews' double from 'The Sound Of Music' in a brightly colored summer dress. I mean, Sister Janet was *beautiful*. And young. Like I said, think Julie Andrews. And sweet, and cooperative, and enthusiastic.

We talked for hours. What a story! She wanted me to meet cops she worked with, and gang leaders, and social workers, and schoolteachers.

And so I did.

Each of them added to the legend of Sister Janet. They told me of the families she helped, the kids she kept out of gangs, the rumbles that she broke up, the bullets that whizzed over her head, the turf, the street, the cops, the wounded, and the dead.

And this young, beautiful Julie Andrews look-alike, in her sweatshirt, jeans, and white tennis, would run through the streets and alleys, getting between the gangs, and forcing them to shoot her first if they're going to shoot each other.

****

I started to outline the screenplay. And then came the most incredible event yet. One of the guys I was interviewing asked me if I had talked to Casey Cohen yet.

"Who?" I asked.

"Casey Cohen is the social worker that works closest with Sister Janet."

Funny she had never mentioned his name. I got his office phone number, called him, and we set up a meeting for the next day.

Casey was also young. Good-looking. A little bit like a young George Segal.

We, too, talked for hours. I could see he was concerned.

"I worry about her," he told me. "She's so innocent. So forgiving. I sometimes wonder if she realizes the danger she puts herself in."

"Maybe God watches out for her because she's so special."

He smiled. "She *is* special, isn't she?"

I nodded in agreement.

He sighed. "I'm so in love with her."

I sighed. "So am I. I mean, who isn't?"

"No," he said. "I mean really in love."

"Hell," I cut in, "we all are."

"And she loves me. Nobody knows this but we sleep together."

My god, I said to myself, *he's delusional.*

"At night, after everyone's asleep, I sneak into their home, go to her room, and with my knees on the floor, we lie next to each other until we fall asleep. In the early morning I sneak out before anyone awakens."

He paused. "Can you use that in your movie?"

"Use it?! It's sensational! But, can I check with Sister Janet first?"

He smiled. "Of course. I wouldn't want you to use it without her permission."

That night she and I met. She was wearing a sports jacket with some high school's basketball team's logo.

"I met Casey Cohen today."

"Oh?"

I was playing it cagey. "How come you never told me about him?"

"Didn't I?" She was playing it cagey with me, too.

"He says the two of you are . . ." I searched for the right words. "He says you're very close."

She knew what I meant.

"His knees are always on the floor. We whisper to each other so as to not wake anyone. We talk until we fall asleep."

"Who knows?"

"No one."

"I'd . . . I'd like to use this in my script. But . . . will it get you in trouble?"

"We have done nothing to be ashamed of. What I feel for Casey does not change my responsibilities or my love of God. There is room in my heart for both."

****

So I go and write the screenplay. And NBC loves it. There was only one provision. That Mother Superior must approve of the script before filming can start.

Mother Superior hated the script. She told us if we didn't take out the 'sordid and ludicrous' relationship between Sister Janet and Mr. Cohen, she could not give her approval.

NBC said there was no deal without the 'love story.'

I called the Mother Superior. She wouldn't talk to me.

I called Sister Janet. One of the other nuns got on the phone.

"She's not here," she told me.

"Will you have her call me when she gets in?"

But she never does.

All the attempts to talk to Mother Superior were frustratingly futile. And I never heard from Sister Janet again.

The one I heard from is Casey Cohen.

"Well you've fucked up my life. Thanks a lot!"

"Casey, I'm sorry. But . . . where was this relationship going? I mean, for openers, you are Jewish and she's---"

"I know what she is!" He was getting pissed. "Have you heard from her?" he asked.

"No. You?"

"No."

I never heard from Casey again either. And NBC dropped the project.

But before we move on, I've got to tell you two quick Sister Janet stories.

****

While I was writing the screenplay I was living in Las Vegas. I was creative head of TransWorld Productions. We were presently editing the Jerry Vale TV show. So I had time to work on Sister Janet's story.

One day I got a call from her. She was coming to Vegas for a couple of days to visit friends, and would I have time to see her.

"Are you kidding?! I'll *make* time. Let me show you around."

So we made a date. I picked her up at this house where these nuns lived, behind one of the many churches in Vegas, and took her to Caesar's Palace for dinner.

She looked fantastic. No one would believe this gorgeous lady was a nun.

In the lobby I showed her where the prostitutes hung out to pick up guys, and the plainclothes cops hung out (mostly to protect the prostitutes), and the eye in the sky so that security could monitor the gambling tables.

After diner, I took her into the casino. She was overwhelmed by the sights and the sounds.

"Okay Kenneth, could I have a quarter to play this . . . What did you call it?!"

"It's a one-armed bandit. Pull down on that arm, watch the symbols spin by, and if they stop on a winning combination you can win up to $25,000."

I gave her a quarter. She lost.

"Can I have another?" she asked.

I went to get a roll of quarters.

Thirty dollars later and she was hooked. Her eyes spat fire. Her teeth were clenched. Anger! Determination! Fury!

Quarter after quarter down the drain. I saw a Sister Janet I had never seen before. Sweet, demure, innocent Sister Janet smacked the one-armed bandit and defiantly cried out, "I will beat you. I will not give in. No machine will get the better of me! I want my money!"

I was shocked!

And then, she looked over at me shyly and with that damn wonderful smile of hers she added, "For the church, of course."

$****$

The other story had to do with when I finished my first script draft and sent a copy to Sister Janet as a courtesy. The next day she called me in Vegas and said, "Oh, Kenneth, I read the script last night, it's wonderful. I love it."

I was beaming.

"And this morning," she continued, "I went into the chapel to pray and ask for God's guidance on the project." There was a pause. Then she added, "And he wants changes on pages 32, 57, and 91!"

Tiffanie DiDonato

TIFFANIE DIDONATO WAS a little person, a dwarf. But to me she was the girl next door; cute and perky, always smiling, always upbeat. Truly, a living doll.

When she graduated college back east her mother told her, as a graduation gift, she'd take her anywhere in the world on vacation.

But she told her mother, "I want to go to L.A. and study writing with a guy named Ken Rotcop."

And so they did.

✶✶✶✶

For a couple of weeks, Tiff and I met every day. At night, she'd come to one of my workshops, or she and her mom and my wife and I would go out to dinner.

She had come to Los Angeles with the screenplay she had written about a high-school coed who, one-by-one, murdered all her teachers.

The script was dreadful. Forget believable.

"Tiffanie, why did you write this story?" I asked.

She hesitated a moment, then told this most incredible story.

"Well," she started, "that was my fantasy. I really wanted to kill all my teachers."

"Why?"

"They were mean to me. Made fun of me. Treated me like I was dirt."

"Your teachers? All of them?"

"And, of course, that gave permission for the kids to treat me the same way. I was miserable. I couldn't wait to get out of there."

"But you went on to college."

"Not right away. If school was torture that was nothing compared to what I did the next two years of my life."

"What?" I was thinking of her being bullied, laughed at, ridiculed, and made fun of just because she was a little person, by her smart-assed peers and prejudicial teachers.

"I told my mother I could not go on living my life. I was tired of carrying a stool around so I could reach the sink or the light switch or a doorknob. I couldn't put on earrings. My arms weren't long enough.

"I told her I wanted to stretch my body."

Of course, being a comic book junkie as a kid, I immediately envisioned Plastic Man, a superhero who could elongate his arms even around corners to catch the bad guys trying to escape!

Tiffanie found a doctor who would help her, though he questioned the procedure himself.

He could guarantee three inches, but Tiffanie wanted more. "I can wear high heels and be three inches taller," she told the doctor.

So, against his better judgment, they started the procedure. It meant sawing the bones of her legs. Then metal braces would be wrapped around her limbs to align the bones. Every day Tiffanie would separate the bones a millimeter at a time by turning screws in both legs.

The hope was that the bones that had been separated would grow towards each other, filling in the gap, and effectively lengthening the legs.

The pain was excruciating. Tiffanie's father could hardly watch the suffering Tiffanie was enduring. But her mother stood by her side with every turning of the screw and gave Tiffanie the strength to go on with the procedure.

Tiffanie stretched her body an unprecedented 14 inches! Once, her height was 3'8". Tiffanie was now 4'10" tall.

"No longer would I be the butt of everyone's jokes or the victim of their pranks. I was literally a new person. I began to gain confidence, believe in myself. I learned to drive, cook on the stove, and take out the trash. I'd wished my grandma and grandpa could see me now."

"They are both dead?" I asked.

"No, they are around. Only. . ." She sighed. This wasn't going to be easy. "When I was born and the doctor told my parents I was going to be a dwarf, my dad's parents told my mother and father to get rid of me right away, that my parents didn't need the grief and heartache of bringing up a freak-of-nature.

"They said if my parents decided to keep me that they would have nothing to do with me and would never see me.

"My mom refused to give me up. And so to this day I've never met my grandparents."

We were both silent for a long moment.

Then, I blurted out, "Tiffanie, forget the girl who kills all her teachers. *This* is the story you must write. The story of your life. It's incredible."

✷✷✷✷

And so we started. Tiffanie kept talking. There were the doctors who turned her down, said no one had ever been stretched more than 3 inches; the one boy in school who actually became her best friend before he committed suicide; the torment of high school; her mother who never left Tiffanie's side; her father who had to choose between his parents or his wife and his weirdo baby; and finally the college life where she was the most popular girl in her sorority.

And when she finished talking we knew Tiffanie had a book to write and a story to tell.

Tiffanie and her mother went back to Boston. Tiff found a collaborator and an agent and a major publisher and you can buy her book. It's called "Dwarf" by Tiffanie DiDonato.

But that's not the end of the story.

✳✳✳✳

It was sometime in late November. Tiffanie read about all the soldiers and Marines stationed in Afghanistan who were going to miss Christmas.

So she got an idea. Buy a few goodies, wrap them in an old sock, and send them to one of the boys over there.

She told her friends. They decided to send socks too. They told other friends. Soon, a whole neighborhood was filling old socks. A reporter from one of the Boston newspapers heard the story.

She interviewed Tiffanie. People read the story and started sending Tiffanie rolled up socks filled with Christmas presents.

Word spread. Now all of New England got involved.

Now mail sacks and more mail sacks of rolled up socks brought by the post office ended up in Tiffanie's living room. Tiffanie's mother declared, "I can't afford to send these to Afghanistan! We'll go broke!"

One of the overseas carriers heard about Tiffanie's plight and offered to deliver each and every rolled up sock, no charge!

And so hundreds and hundreds of soldiers and Marines received rolled up Christmas socks with presents from the people of New England.

And that is *still* not the end of Tiffanie's story!

✳✳✳✳

Many of the soldiers and Marines wrote to Tiffanie to thank her. A lot of them kept up a correspondence with her for many, many months.

But one young man, a Marine, discovered through their writing to each other, he and Tiffanie had a lot in common. A love for books. And movies. And theater.

And through their writings they began to bond.

When he wrote he was coming home, back to the States, and wanted to meet her, she was at first ecstatic, and then suddenly filled with trepidation.

She ran to her mother. "Mom, what should I do? He doesn't know I'm a dwarf. What should I tell him? Or should I lie and tell him I'm engaged or married or---"

"Tell him the truth. Give him the choice. If he can't handle it, better to find out now."

She told him and held her breath until he replied, "Here's my flight information. Will I see you at the airport?"

When he arrived at Logan Airport, Tiffanie watched from the tarmac as battle-weary Marines bounded down the plane's ramp. Her heart was pounding so fast in that little body she thought she would faint.

He spotted her, ran to her, swooped her up in his arms, and spun her around and around while tears welled in both their eyes.

"How'd you know it was me?" she asked. They both giggled through their tears.

****

Now, the kicker. Tiffanie and Eric, the six-foot tall, handsome Marine, are married and have a son who is as normal as apple pie. After attending their wedding in Maine, Tiffanie sent me a thank you letter and ended it by saying I was the grandfather she never had.

And that script about the girl who killed all her teachers? It sits on a shelf somewhere, hopefully never to see the light of day.

Barbra Streisand & Burt Reynolds

BY FAR THE strangest story I ever got involved in was over the script titled 'Squaw Dance.'

****

Avco-Embassy was closing.

Sure we had made three blockbuster movies with 'The Graduate,' 'Carnal Knowledge,' and 'The Lion In Winter.'

But just as Joseph E. Levine, my boss, thought he was invulnerable, that he had the Midas touch, and that every movie that started with "Joseph E. Levine Presents" would bring in huge profits, the roof caved in.

Joe went to Europe and began buying up every foreign film he could get his hands on. Twenty in all. And they all bombed here in the States.

Jim Kerr, president of Avco, had enough. He stopped the bleeding and threw us all out, including Levine.

But, before I left I was given some nice parting gifts. One was that I could take any script the company owned and they would turn the rights over to me.

I picked a script I loved titled 'Squaw Dance.'

I was immediately able to make a deal for seed money at 20th

Century Fox. They gave me an office, a secretary, and I was in business.

I did two things simultaneously. Got the script to the great director Marty Ritt, who had made 'Norma Rae,' 'Hud,' 'The Long Hot Summer,' and many other hit films, and also contacted the writer of the screenplay, Judy Barrow.

✳✳✳✳

Judy lived with her husband Bob on a ranch in a place called Cuba, New Mexico.

I told her Marty Ritt loved the script, wanted to direct the movie, and had a few notes for her.

We flew Judy and her husband Bob in for a meeting with the great director.

I'd say that the Barrows were in their 40s. She was plump and Jewish. He was thin and not Jewish.

Judy's story was about a Beverly Hills Jewish lady who leaves her husband and, on a whim, buys a log cabin somewhere in, yes, New Mexico.

Turns out the log cabin is right smack in the middle of an Indian reservation and she learns the way of Indian customs and tradition and the Indians learn the ways of Beverly Hills.

She also falls in love with the local good ol' boy Sheriff. When her husband finds out where she is, he comes to New Mexico to get her back.

The story had a lot of relevance, poignancy, and comedy, and Judy had done a wonderful job writing the screenplay.

But something my new secretary said to me after she had read the script has stuck with me to this day.

"She's crying out for help, you know," she advised me.

"Who? The character?"

"No. The writer. Judy Barrows. She wants to be helped."

Now, before the secretary came to work for me she was a production assistant on the soap opera 'Peyton Place.' I told her she was being overdramatic, that she had soap-opera-on-the-brain.

But I never forgot how adamant she was.

I have to tell you how Judy's screenplay ends. The Beverly Hills lady realizes she doesn't want to leave her husband even though she loves the Sheriff. She races out of town in her Rolls Royce convertible, but is chased by the Sheriff, who wants her back, in his patrol car.

With red lights flashing and sirens wailing, he tries to catch up to her. She looks back, misses a turn, crashes! End of Beverly Hills lady. End of story.

So maybe there was enough evidence for my secretary's forewarning.

✳✳✳✳

Anyway, Judy, her husband and I met with Marty Ritt. His notes were minor. Very easy to edit into the script.

More importantly Marty was a kindly, warm man, in his late 50s I would guess, and he quickly took a liking to Judy and offered to make himself available to her any time.

And then I threw in my two cents.

"If Marty's on board then I have two announcements to make." I had everybody's attention. "I sat with Barbra Streisand at her home and she committed to play the Beverly Hills lady. And I went to Burt Reynolds' house and he committed to play the Sheriff!"

Now everybody was excited. It sounded like perfect casting.

Unfortunately, here is where it all begins to fall apart.

That night I went out to dinner with Judy and Bob. "Sorry, Ken, I can't do it." That was the first of Judy's bombshells.

"What are you talking about?" I asked.

"I can't do the rewrite Marty wants."

"Of course you can. It's easy stuff. I'll help you. Hell, Marty'll help you."

"It won't work. You'll be disappointed."

"What are you talking about?" At this point I'm not worried, because most writers have trepidations when they're trying to impress someone as important as Marty Ritt.

"He reminds me of my father and I was never able to satisfy my father. My father was a kind man, a caring man to everyone but me. Whatever I did it wasn't good enough. I'm going home. Forget 'Squaw Dance.' It's not going to happen."

She sipped some water.

"Look," I say, "take a few days off, go shopping in Beverly Hills, go sightseeing in Hollywood, go to some really good restaurants, go to a movie, then at the end of the week, we'll sit down and see how you feel."

She said she'd think on it.

****

Three days go by. Then the second bombshell.

A call from husband Bob.

"Ken? Bad news. Judy committed suicide."

"What?!"

"She drove out to the cemetery where her father is buried, pulled over at his headstone, took an overdose of pills, and killed herself."

There was my secretary's voice ringing in my ears. "She's crying out for help, you know."

****

Less than three weeks later, Bob Barrows was back in Cuba, New Mexico, and took out a full-page ad in the Hollywood Reporter and, I believe, Daily Variety as well.

It read something like this:

"Because of my wife's death all rights to her screenplay 'Squaw Dance' revert back to me, her husband.

"Ken Rotcop has no ownership to the material and to deal with him would be illegal, reprehensible, and punishable.

"For further information contact Robert Barrows at blah, blah, blah . . ."

20th Century Fox said they couldn't afford to get entangled in possible lawsuits and backed off as the financier.

Marty Ritt went on to direct 'The Great White Hope.'

Streisand's agent put her in 'Up The Sandbox.' A terrible movie.

Burt Reynolds left to do some TV shows.

But damnit, I wasn't giving up that easily.

I called Barrows on the phone.

"Bob, I'm coming out to New Mexico to talk to you. I'm arriving in Albuquerque tomorrow. Pick me up."

Here comes the next bombshell.

****

He met me at the airport in an old, beat-up truck and he, this young girl, and I squeezed into the front seat.

He introduced me to the girl, who I thought might be his daughter. Turned out she was a student at a local college, used to clean Barrow's house to make some extra money, and Bob had gone and *married her!*

Bob Barrows had a new wife!

I spent three days with the Barrows, his new wife, and his kids (the oldest boy was about the same age as his new wife).

We smoked, we drank, we went swimming in the nude, we went horseback riding, and in those moments when Barrows was sober, we talked about Judy and 'Squaw Dance.'

After three intense days and nights, drinking more cans of beer than I had had in my lifetime, with an improving nod from the new wife, Barrows gave me back 'Squaw Dance.'

✶✶✶✶

Back in L.A., I started all over again. Only now, the project was tainted.

Couldn't get Dave Gershenson on the phone. He was Burt Reynolds' manager.

Couldn't get Sue Mengers on the phone. She was Barbra Streisand's agent.

Couldn't get Richard Zanuck on the phone. He ran 20th Century Fox.

I tried to get Barrows to take out a second full-page ad in the trade paper denouncing the first ad.

He wouldn't do it.

So, after every studio turned me down I returned the property to Barrows and wished him good luck.

Now for the final bombshell.

****

Two or three years go by and I'm on to other things. There's some kind of event at the Writers Guild that I attend.

And who did I meet there but Bob Barrows and the wife.

"Still in Cuba, New Mexico?"

"Yep. Just in for a vacation."

"Bob, whatever happened with 'Squaw Dance'?

"I just sold it."

"To who?"

"Colossus Films."

"Great," I exclaim. "Can I ask you for how much?"

"Twenty thou."

I think, *Twenty thou?* Judy was going to get over a hundred thou from 20th Century Fox and I think Avco Embassy paid her thirty. Yet Barrows was beaming. He was thrilled to get the twenty.

That wasn't the bombshell. What happened next was.

****

The next day I look up Colossus Films. Their address is on Sunset Boulevard in Hollywood.

So I go there.

What did I expect to accomplish? I didn't know. But 'Squaw Dance' was like an ol' friend. Maybe I could renew acquaintances.

Colossus had offices in the Playboy building.

I looked them up on the lobby directory, took an elevator up to their floor, found the door number, and entered the office.

There were movie posters on every wall. I was definitely in the right place.

I asked the receptionist who her boss was and told her I'd like to talk to him.

"What's it in reference to?" she asked, looking up from reading a romance novel while chewing gum.

I tell her it's about a script titled 'Squaw Dance.' She buzzed him and then told me, "He'll be right out."

I looked around at the movie posters. And I realized that, one, they all starred the same blonde bombshell who I had never heard of and, two, they were all hard-core pornography!

Bob Barrows sold 'Squaw Dance,' this beautiful, sensitive, sweet story to a porno house!

This guy came out, we shook hands, and he invited me into his office.

His first question was, "How do you know about 'Squaw Dance'?"

I told him the whole story.

Then he told me his.

The 'actress' in all those posters was his wife. Somewhere, somehow, she found 'Squaw Dance.' She wanted her husband to make the movie. It was her chance to break out of porn. She would play the Beverly Hills wife who leaves her husband and moves to an Indian reservation in New Mexico.

So the husband told me he bought the script from Barrows and he kept dangling 'Squaw Dance' like a carrot over his porno wife. He kept telling her that if she made just a couple more pornos, he'd make 'Squaw Dance.'

But he confided to me that he had no intention of ever making 'Squaw Dance.' It was just a way to keep his wife working.

"You want to sell the rights to me?" I asked.

"Hell, no. The script has paid for itself ten times over with the films my wife keeps making!"

When I left he gave me three DVDs of movies he had made with her.

In the lobby I tossed them all into a receptacle and left the building.

Well . . . Maybe I kept one.

As a memento.

$$****$$

And, as I was walking to my car, I was talking to Judy Barrows. "Sorry, Judy, I wish I could've done better for you. If only you hadn't . . . you know."

About the Author

KEN ROTCOP HAS won the Writers Guild Award, The Neil Simon Award, and the Image Award for writing and producing the television movie 'For Us, The Living: The Story Of Medgar Evers.'

He was also the recipient of the Unity Award for writing the best television documentary series 'Images of America' for CBS.

He has been creative head of four studios: Hanna-Barbera, Avco Embassy Pictures, Cannon Films, and TransWorld Productions.

He is the author of the best selling series of books 'The Perfect Pitch: How To Sell Yourself And Your Movie Idea To Hollywood.' His four DVDs on writing, pitching, and selling your scripts are in bookstores and colleges everywhere.

He presently hosts a writers' workshop in Los Angeles and is a guest speaker at colleges, writers' groups, actors' studios and on cruise ships.

He lives in Woodland Hills, California with his wife Connie and yorkie Kady.

For more information on Ken's workshops and website go to www.pitchmart.com or email Ken at pitchmart@gmail.com.

About the Artist

ARIEL ECHEVARRIA IS a member of the ISCA, the International Society of Caricature Artists. He is a freelance artist and caricaturist living in the Detroit, Michigan area.

He attended The Center for Creative Studies in Detroit, where he majored in Graphic Communication and first started to develop his caricaturing and cartooning style.

Clocking in at about 3-5 minutes per face, he averages about 2,000 caricatures per year at various parties and private events for everyone from Fortune 500 companies to birthday parties and wedding receptions.

'As I Best Remember It: From Marilyn To Streisand And All The Celebs In Between' is Ariel's second venture into the book publishing world.

He dedicates his sketches in the book to his daughter Elena. Ariel may be reached atariel@ariel-view.com www.facebook.com/arielview90.

www.ingramcontent.com/pod-product-compliance
Lightning Source LLC
Chambersburg PA
CBHW070758100426
42742CB00012B/2181